RSF: The Russell Sage Foundation Journal of the Social Sciences

Big Data in Political Economy

VOLUME 2 · NUMBER 7 · NOVEMBER 2016

RSF: The Russell Sage Foundation Journal of the Social Sciences ISSN 2377-8261

The Russell Sage Foundation

The Russell Sage Foundation, one of the oldest of America's general purpose foundations, was established in 1907 by Mrs. Margaret Olivia Sage for "the improvement of social and living conditions in the United States." The foundation seeks to fulfill this mandate by fostering the development and dissemination of knowledge about the country's political, social, and economic problems. While the foundation endeavors to assure the accuracy and objectivity of each book it publishes, the conclusions and interpretations in Russell Sage Foundation publications are those of the authors and not of the foundation, its trustees, or its staff. Publication by Russell Sage, therefore, does not imply foundation endorsement.

Board of Trustees

Sara S. McLanahan, *Chair*
Larry M. Bartels
Karen S. Cook
W. Bowman Cutter III
Sheldon H. Danziger
Kathryn Edin
Lawrence F. Katz
David Laibson
Nicholas Lemann
Martha Minow
Peter R. Orszag
Claude M. Steele
Shelley E. Taylor
Richard H. Thaler
Hirokazu Yoshikawa

Mission Statement

RSF: The Russell Sage Foundation Journal of the Social Sciences is a peer-reviewed, open-access journal of original empirical research articles by both established and emerging scholars. It is designed to promote cross-disciplinary collaborations on timely issues of interest to academics, policymakers, and the public at large. Each issue is thematic in nature and focuses on a specific research question or area of interest. The introduction to each issue will include an accessible, broad, and synthetic overview of the research question under consideration and the current thinking from the various social sciences.

RSF Journal Editorial Board

Elizabeth O. Ananat, Duke University
Annette Bernhardt, University of California, Berkeley
Karen S. Cook, Stanford University
Sheldon H. Danziger, RSF President
Janet C. Gornick, The CUNY Graduate Center
Jennifer Hochschild, Harvard University
Douglas S. Massey, Princeton University
Mary E. Pattillo, Northwestern University
James Sidanius, Harvard University
Mary C. Waters, Harvard University
Bruce Western, Harvard University

Copyright © 2016 by Russell Sage Foundation. All rights reserved. Printed in the United States of America. No part of this publication may be reproduced, stored in a retrieval system, or transmitted in any form or by any means, electronic, mechanical, photocopying, recording, or otherwise, without the prior written permission of the publisher. Reproduction by the United States Government in whole or in part is permitted for any purpose.

Opinions expressed in this journal are not necessarily those of the editors, editorial board, trustees, or the Russell Sage Foundation.

We invite scholars to submit proposals for potential issues through the *RSF* application portal: https://rsfjournal.onlineapplicationportal.com/. Submissions should be addressed to Suzanne Nichols, Director of Publications.

To view the complete text and additional features online please go to **www.rsfjournal.org**.

Russell Sage Foundation
112 East 64th Street
New York, NY 10065

ISSN (print): 2377-8253
ISSN (electronic): 2377-8261
ISBN: 978-0-87154-730-9

Big Data in Political Economy

RSF: The Russell Sage Foundation Journal of the Social Sciences

VOLUME 2 NUMBER 7
NOVEMBER 2016

ISSUE EDITORS
Atif Mian, Princeton University
Howard Rosenthal, New York University

CONTENTS

Introduction: Big Data in Political Economy **1**
Atif Mian and Howard Rosenthal

A Data-Driven Voter Guide for U.S. Elections: Adapting Quantitative Measures of the Preferences and Priorities of Political Elites to Help Voters Learn About Candidates **11**
Adam Bonica

Income, Ideology, and Representation **33**
Chris Tausanovitch

Shining the Light on Dark Money: Political Spending by Nonprofits **51**
Drew Dimmery and Andrew Peterson

Home Truths: Promises and Challenges in Linking Mortgages and Political Influence **69**
Deniz Igan

Data Science and Political Economy: Application to Financial Regulatory Structure **87**
Sharyn O'Halloran, Sameer Maskey, Geraldine McAllister, David K. Park, and Kaiping Chen

Introduction: Big Data in Political Economy

ATIF MIAN AND HOWARD ROSENTHAL

The massive growth in computing since the 1980s and 1990s has revolutionized data gathering and how people transact with one another. The result is that practically every economic and financial transaction is recorded somewhere by someone and can be linked to the individuals undertaking the transaction. Such proliferation of "big data" has made it possible for both economists and political scientists to empirically analyze questions that earlier could be addressed only theoretically. In particular, big data permits us to study behavior at both a high level of disaggregation and a high time frequency. For example, what is a household's spending behavior and how does it depend on changes in interest rates, asset prices, or political events? How do households form expectations of future events? How do ideology and electoral politics affect these expectations? What are the distributional consequences of macro shocks—such as the impact of monetary policy or housing collapse on the rich versus the poor? These are fundamental economic and political questions that can now be addressed using advancements in data collection and computing.

BIG DATA: WHAT IS NEW AND DISTINCTIVE

There are numerous examples of research using new, disaggregated data sources, several appearing in this issue. These include data on mortgage originators (Igan, this issue); national data on individual voter registration and turnout (Catalist); data on the characteristics of individual professionals such as medical doctors (Bonica, Rothman, and Rosenthal 2014, 2015) or lawyers (Bonica, Chilton, and Sen 2015); government payments to contractors; Medicare payments to physicians; pharmaceutical company payments to physicians; campaign contributions (Bonica, this issue; Dimmery and Peterson, this issue); lobbying (Igan, this issue); tariffs (Kim 2014); traditional and social media content; government documents (O'Halloran et al., this issue); Google searches (Chae et al. 2015); and Twitter followers (Barberá 2015).

Of course, for big data to be seen as transforming research in political economy, it must be more than just the analysis of data sets with very large numbers of observations. Researchers have been exploiting the census for decades. Similarly, the pathbreaking research of Thomas Piketty and Emmanuel Saez (2003), using individual IRS records, dates from the turn of the century. In the 1980s, Keith Poole and Howard Rosenthal (1991) studied the entire congressional history of tens of millions of individual roll call voting decisions with a supercomputer. So what is distinctive about the current use of "big data" in political econ-

Atif Mian is Theodore A. Wells '29 Professor of Economics and Public Affairs at Princeton University. **Howard Rosenthal** is professor of politics at New York University and Roger Williams Straus Professor of Social Sciences, Emeritus, at Princeton University.

Direct correspondence to: Atif Mian at atif@princeton.edu, 26 Prospect Ave., Princeton, NJ 08540; and Howard Rosenthal at hr31@nyu.edu, NYU Department of Politics, 19 W. 4th St., New York, NY 10012.

omy? At least the following considerations appear relevant[1]:

1. *A new ability to link large data sets that are of far more limited use if unlinked* has emerged. For example, political activity in the form of lobbying can be linked to microlevel data on the firm's business activity, such as mortgage lending behavior in metropolitan statistical areas (see Igan, this issue). Another example is political activity in the form of roll call voting by a member of Congress, which can now be linked not just to aggregate economic characteristics such as median income but more finely to characteristics of small geographic units in congressional districts, such as mortgage foreclosure activity in portions of the district that have a high level of Republican voting (Mian, Sufi, and Trebbi 2010).

An important aspect of record linkage is the development of automated record linkage through the use of algorithms that assign a probability that a record from one data set can be matched to another. Record linkage is also facilitated by geocoding techniques. Researchers are recognizing that matches must carry an acceptable level of measurement error but need not be perfect. For example, political activity in the form of campaign contributions can be linked to the professional and demographic characteristics of individuals in most licensed professions (medicine, law, nursing) or state government employment and in some cases to income data (state government employees, including academics and physicians in university hospitals). More recently, researchers have been able to link public records such as bankruptcy filings (for example, Dobbie and Song 2015) with Social Security data to address questions like the impact of debtor relief on earnings and labor supply. Atif Mian, Amir Sufi, and Nasim Khoshkhou (2016) link constituent ideology and voting outcomes with consumer spending at the county level and with individual survey data on consumer sentiments to analyze the link between consumer spending and sentiments about government policy.

2. *A growing ability to extract data directly from web pages,* using Python and other tools, has become an important source of additional data. For example, Matthew Gentzkow and Jesse Shapiro (2010) use textual analysis of online newspaper data to construct measures of "slant" in various newspapers.

3. *The growth of computing capacity* remains important. For example, Chris Tausanovitch (this issue) carries out an ideological scaling using hundreds of thousands of public opinion surveys. The scaling takes advantage of special software that uses graphics chips to turn PCs into parallel processors. Changes in estimation strategy are also likely to accompany the use of big data. For example, Kosuke Imai, James Lo, and Jonathan Olmsted (2015) have recently proposed using efficient expectation-maximization (EM) algorithms for ideological scaling to replace the widely used Markov chain Monte Carlo (MCMC) methods. Computing capacity and estimation strategy are likely to be particularly important in the growing area of text analysis, as illustrated by O'Halloran and her colleagues in this issue.

4. *The private sector has become a large provider of big data* of potential usefulness to political economists. Big data about financial markets have been available for many years, accessible to academics through Wharton Research Data Services (WRDS) and other sources. More recently, data have begun to be accumulated about career paths (LinkedIn) and about housing and consumer markets. The private sector both complements and substitutes for the government sector. For example, LinkedIn can provide data about workers in unlicensed professions that can comple-

---

1. The software firm SAS characterizes big data as having volume, velocity, variety, variability, and complexity. See SAS, "Big Data: What It Is and Why It Matters," http://www.sas.com/en_us/insights/big-data/what-is-big-data.html?keyword=big%20data&matchtype=e&publisher=google&gclid=CjwKEAiAxfu1BRDF2cfnoPyB9jESJADF-MdJlJyvsnTWDXHchganXKpdoer1lb_DpSy6IW_pZUTE_hoCCwDw_wcB (accessed February 13, 2016). "Velocity" and "variability" refer to real-time applications, which are not yet present in political economy. The papers in this issue represent applications that have large volumes of data, data arising in different formats, and data with complex structures.

ment the data in government databases about those in licensed professions.

The growth of online payment and personal finance tools has given researchers access to people's spending and investing behavior. For example, Scott Baker (2014) uses data from individual accounts at a personal finance site to investigate how consumers respond to income shocks in the presence of debt. Mian, Rao, and Sufi (2013) use data on credit card spending to analyze the impact of the housing collapse on spending. Similar data have been used to analyze the impact of political shocks—as when the federal government approached the fiscal cliff or when it was threatened with shutdown—on consumer spending behavior as well.

A related feature of these data is that they are potentially available at high frequency, such as daily spending behavior. The high frequency enables researchers to exploit the sharp timing of certain events—such as the fall of Lehman Brothers in September 2008 or the attacks of September 11, 2001—to analyze the impact on consumer spending and investment behavior.

Credit bureaus, both in the United States and abroad, are another important private source of data. The credit bureaus contain data on all types of borrowing at the individual level at monthly frequency. These data also contain information on an individual's location and basic demographics and are thus potentially linkable to other data sets. Mian and Sufi (2014) describe a number of examples of research studies using credit bureau data.

A number of private firms specialize in collecting and consolidating data from a large number of public data sources. For example, the Securities and Exchange Commission (SEC) requires publicly traded corporations to file a variety of reports, including information on trading by insiders and on large block holdings. Since 1993, this information has been available in electronic form on the SEC's EDGAR platform. But the SEC has done little to summarize these reports in a way that would be useful to researchers. One cannot go to the SEC site and download a spreadsheet with the details of the largest owners of S&P 1500 companies. On the other hand, firms like Vickers Stock Research have such data in more accessible forms.

5. *Government electronic record keeping has also expanded dramatically.* About the time the SEC created EDGAR, for example, government agencies in the fifty states, such as education departments, were shifting to electronic, web-accessible data. Records that were previously accessible only as copied or scanned documents became available in spreadsheet form. A transition to transparency has accompanied the technological transition to electronic record keeping.

Data on government payments to most contractors have long been a matter of public record, but the provision to the public of information on government payments to health care providers, long resisted by the providers, did not become federal government policy until 2014. Similarly, disclosure of payments to providers by pharmaceutical companies was required by the Physician Payments Sunshine Act, a part of the Affordable Care Act passed in 2010.

There have also been important shifts in the availability of large individual-level data sets at various governmental organizations. For example, academics have worked with the Internal Revenue Service (IRS) on tax return data and the Social Security Administration (SSA) on payroll data. These data have been extremely useful in illuminating trends in inequality and social mobility. At the same time, the granularity of the data sets is useful in helping us better understand the impact of changes in tax laws and other public policy interventions. The U.S. Census Bureau also maintains data on sales and employees by firm.

6. At the same time, *the development of optical character recognition (OCR) made it possible to process older data at relatively low cost.* Ten years ago, analysis of roll call voting data was largely limited to the U.S. Congress. Boris Shor and Nolan McCarty (2011) have extended this work to all fifty states.

THE CHALLENGES OF BIG DATA

The use of big data does present some challenges for academic research. There are questions of data accuracy. There is a question of equal access to data. There is a question of the ethics of the relationship of academic researchers to private-sector collectors of data. Although the challenges we identify apply more generally to the social sciences, political economy faces some particularly intensive challenges: because political economy addresses the interplay between political transactions and market transactions, the need for market transaction data makes political economists heavily dependent on the private sector.

Data Accuracy

There are several potential problems with respect to data accuracy:

What Inferences Can Be Made from the Sampling Universe?

This question is particularly relevant for data from search engines and social media. Are individuals who search on Google representative of the larger population? Are heavy searchers representative of all searchers? Are Twitter users representative of broader population? Some of the data in the Tausanovitch paper in this issue come from surveys conducted through the Internet. In longitudinal studies, how will these data match up with data collected in the 1950s through door-to-door interviews or with telephone interviews in the 1990s?

Campaign contributions, explored in the Bonica paper in this issue, allow us to study groups that are not reported in sample surveys. For example, medical doctors would represent only on the order of 1 percent of the respondents in a survey of 2,000 adult Americans. But 145,000 physicians have made campaign contributions, with an indication of partisan preference, over the past twenty years (Bonica et al. 2014, 2015). Those 145,000 physicians, in turn, can be broken down into still large samples by specialty, gender, and employer type. But are these 145,000 representative of the nearly 900,000 physicians in the United States?

Another larger source of partisan preference could come from voter registration data put together by Catalist. The Catalist data have also been used to study physician preferences about patient management (Hersh and Goldenberg 2016). Again, are physicians who are registered voters representative of physicians? Are former government employees with LinkedIn accounts representative of all former government employees?

A related big data development is represented by attempts to "bridge" different sampling universes by using common stimuli—for example, a legislative roll call vote on a bill and media editorials on the same bill. Jeffrey Lewis and Chris Tausanovitch (2015) survey this literature and discuss its promises and shortcomings.

Record linkage introduces inaccuracy. In the case of campaign contributions to candidates, the reports of individual candidates may be prepared by unpaid interns who lack strong incentives to be accurate. Even when the initial reports are filed accurately, reports across candidates can have a different name spelling and address for the same individual. Conversely, individuals with common last names can be confused. When the contributors are linked to another database, such as the National Provider Identifier (NPI) database that the government maintains for physicians, there is further opportunity for mismatch.

New Sources of Big Data May Contain Misrepresentation

Misrepresentation is hardly a new problem. For instance, the November Current Population Survey (CPS) has long been used to study voter turnout (Wolfinger and Rosenstone 1980), but turnout is substantially overreported in the CPS. Citizenship is also likely to be overreported (McCarty, Poole, and Rosenthal 2006). Income tax and estate tax returns are subject to fraud. Misrepresentation may be particularly important in loan markets (Griffin and Maturana 2013; Mian and Sufi 2015; Keys, Seru, and Vig 2012). Mian and Sufi (2015) show that income reporting on publicly available Home Mortgage Disclosure Act (HMDA) files was subject to large-scale overstatement by mortgage applicants during the mortgage credit boom of 2002 to 2006. The financial incentives of firms to misreport do, however, represent a new concern.

Data Access

As we previously indicated, much of the new big data is being generated by organizations, both for profit (LinkedIn) and by nonprofits (ProPublica) that charge fees for data access. When an academic researcher uses proprietary data, what are the conditions for replication? Should journals allow publication if the entire data set cannot be made available for replication and further study? When the data are purchased, the purchase agreement may exclude the posting of replication materials.[2]

Government agency rules regarding data access have not been sufficiently streamlined yet. There is natural aversion by government agencies to "sharing" their internal data. The reluctance may be due to the fear of either lawsuits or scrutiny by outsiders of how the agency works. The latter excuse warrants greater transparency, as access might have the beneficial side effect of improving the functioning of some government agencies. Another source of reluctance is pressure from private interests. For example, until recently, such pressure kept Medicare payments to individual physicians from public scrutiny.

A related issue is the ability to link various government data sets, which raises a natural concern about privacy. Data are often anonymized before they are shared with researchers. Although this is a good practice to follow, anonymizing data makes it difficult to link them across different sources. It would be useful if the government came up with a mechanism to link the various data sets before anonymizing them so as to expand the scope of the research that could be conducted using governmental sources of data.

Along similar lines, there is also a need for the government to come up with uniform data access rules across its various agencies. Access to governmental data sometimes depends on who within the agency one knows and can collaborate with. As such, the playing field is not level when it comes to access to government-owned data.

Another question concerns funding: not all academic researchers have the resources to purchase the data in the first place. As government funding for research ebbs—the National Science Foundation (NSF) cut out political science for a period starting in 2013—researchers with large internal research funds, in either professional schools or elite universities, will have an advantage over others. It is also conceivable that private sources of data could grant differential access, essentially limiting access to those individuals whom an organization believes to be "safe." Many private data contracts already give the right of refusal to the data provider in case the provider objects to the research findings.

These important questions regarding access and scientific bias need to be addressed carefully as more and more private data sources are used by academics.

The Ethics of Collaboration

An ethical issue arises when there is an academic collaboration with a for-profit generator of big data. The situation was highlighted by the Facebook deception study in 2014 (Albertson and Gadarian 2014). The study, which involved a researcher from Cornell University, had the "big data" advantage that it was possible to study the behavior of 700,000 individuals. The big data issue is that a private firm, such as Facebook, has proprietary interests and research objectives that can differ from those of a small, on-campus laboratory experiment monitored by a university's institutional review board (IRB). In the case of the Facebook deception experiment, the Cornell IRB approved the study with the argument that it was Facebook, not Cornell, that practiced the deception. The study was published in the prestigious *Proceedings of the National Academy of Sciences*. Certainly some researchers would argue that Cornell and *PNAS* made bad choices. Debate is needed about the wider issue of conflicts of interest generated by the interaction of non-academic data providers and academic research.

---

2. This issue arose with a recent publication (Lucca, Seru, and Trebbi 2014) that analyzed the revolving door. Although Francesco Trebbi, at a Harvard conference in 2013, orally stated that the data were from LinkedIn, the conference paper and the published version did not identify LinkedIn as the data source.

A SUMMARY OF THE PAPERS IN THIS ISSUE

Research in political economy is increasingly focused on the role of money expenditures, as against votes, in shaping the outcomes of elections and policy. These expenditures can take the form of lobbying or campaign expenditures. Three of the papers in this issue—by Adam Bonica, by Drew Dimmery and Andrew Peterson, and by Deniz Igan—focus on political expenditures.

The consequences of political expenditures have been debated in the academic literature (compare Levitt 1994 and Erikson and Palfrey 2000). It is easy to identify cases where massive expenditures came up empty. One example is Michael Huffington's record-breaking personal expenditure of $28 million in his 1994 California Senate race against Diane Feinstein. Another is Sheldon Adelson's $140 million expenditure on the 2012 election, most of which went into Newt Gingrich's attempt to be the Republican presidential nominee. Comcast's attempt to acquire Time-Warner failed in 2015 despite massive lobbying and personal connections to the Obama administration. On the other hand, expenditure by Adelson and others is said to have forced a total alignment between the Republican congressional delegation in the United States and the Netanyahu government in Israel. Similarly, intense lobbying by hedge funds appears to have maintained the carried interest deduction in the 2012 tax bill.

We are, in terms of the research frontier, several steps away from tightly drawing the linkages between expenditures and the outcomes of elections or legislation. Research at this point, including the three papers on the subject in this issue, is more focused on the motivations and characteristics of the makers of political expenditures. At the individual level, what is the connection to income, wealth, and ideology? At the corporate level, what is the connection to firm characteristics, such as the propensity to take risks or to engage in fraud?

In his paper "Income, Ideology, and Representation," Chris Tausanovitch stresses the low level of voter information about the policy stances of their representatives. The electorate's awareness of where unelected candidates stand is quite arguably even lower. Tausanovitch also points to a very weak linkage between the policy preferences of voters in a constituency and the preferences of their representatives in Congress.

In "A Data-Driven Voter Guide for U.S. Elections," Adam Bonica develops a platform for better informing voters about candidates. So the ambition of the Bonica paper is potentially important. The paper exploits government electronic records, computing capacity, the linkage of a variety of different data sources, and text analysis, four of the important big data facets outlined earlier.

The central innovation of the Bonica paper is the use of the big data present in hundreds of millions of campaign contribution records. Informing voters in the United States is inherently a big data problem because of the decentralized aspect of both campaign finance and the political system, which only weakly controls candidate entry. In parliamentary systems, where online voter guides are important, the informational problem largely reduces to presenting the platforms of one or two handfuls of national parties. In the United States, politics can be described in one-dimensional liberal-conservative terms (Poole and Rosenthal 2007), but placing candidates on this continuum is challenging. Most candidates in an election have not previously been elected to a legislature, either because they are new entrants or because they have never won a past election. So their positions cannot be estimated from the well-established methods of roll call vote scaling developed for Congress (Poole and Rosenthal 2007) or state legislatures (Shor and McCarty 2011). But candidates—not only in federal elections but also for state legislatures and elected positions in state courts—can be placed on a common scale using the information provided by campaign contributors. If an individual, for example, contributes to a candidate for a U.S. Senate seat, a state lower house seat, and a judicial contest, the individual's contributions will provide information that glues together the continuum for two legislatures and a judicial body (Bonica 2013, 2014). More information is provided by candidates who, as is most often the case, are also contributors in other races.

To provide context to the contribution data, the platform also incorporates information from political text, election outcomes, and roll call scaling. Use of this additional information allows the platform to provide voters with information on candidate positions on specific issues. In practice, given the unidimensionality of American politics, information on specific issues is attractive in presentation but marginal in terms of information value. Bonica nicely refers to this problem as the "curse of unidimensionality."

Bonica's paper emphasizes the importance of disclosure of campaign contributions and roll call votes in providing information to the public. Disclosure, however, is not always implicit in democracy. Roll call votes in the Italian parliament were secret until 1988 (Giannetti 2010). In the United States, political expenditures by nonprofits—specifically, 501(c) organizations—are subject to minimal disclosure and have become increasingly important. Drew Dimmery and Andrew Peterson, in "Shining the Light on Dark Money," take a big data approach to identifying the political activity and expenditure of 340,000 nonprofits. The paper crosswalks government electronic websites and information from the websites of the nonprofits.

Dimmery and Peterson use automated techniques to identify the websites of nonprofits and then to scrape the websites of the organizations. They argue that the websites reveal more about these organizations than what the organizations report to the federal government or what has previously been gleaned by the Center for Responsive Politics. To ferret out political nonprofits, they match the larger set of nonprofits with a much smaller number of nonprofits whose names or IRS reports directly reveal them to be political organizations and with nearly 11,000 political action committees (PACs) that register with the Federal Election Commission (FEC). Nonprofits are deemed political when their websites use language similar to that used on the websites of known political organizations. The automated sources are validated by human evaluations that are crowdsourced.

The study is an important entry point to bring nondisclosing organizations into the disclosed world explored in the Bonica paper. For example, the websites are likely to identify the officers of the association (see the websites of Planned Parenthood and Crossroads GPS, two organizations mentioned in the paper), who in turn are very likely to have made individual political contributions. Record linkage of this type can "out" the expenditures and ideology of undisclosed nonprofits.

As we discussed earlier, a key challenge in the political economy literature is to draw a tighter connection between political expenditures and legislation or policy. One way to address this challenge is to focus on expenditure in specific industries and investigate the relationship between political spending and legislative impact. Deniz Igan takes this approach, with specific focus on the household credit, or mortgage, industry.

Focusing on the mortgage industry has some natural advantages, from both a political economy and a big data perspective. First, the financial industry is regulated in a number of different ways. The largest players in the mortgage industry—Freddie Mac and Fannie Mae—have heavy mandates from the government. There is thus a natural incentive for the private sector to try to influence the ways in which the industry is regulated. Second, large data are available for analysis, both for campaign contributions and for disbursements of mortgage credit. Igan describes a comprehensive data set on political influence exerted by financial institutions on Congress and links it to the mortgage lending activity of these institutions. She then describes the role of political influence in dictating financial regulation and credit disbursement during the U.S. credit boom of 1999 to 2006.

Results suggest that lobbying by financial institutions helped sway legislative decisions. Legislators who changed their vote in favor of deregulation under various bills were more likely to have been lobbied by the financial industry. At the same time, financial institutions that engaged in greater lobbying of the legislature were more likely to engage in risky lending behavior. For example, financial institutions that spent more on lobbying activity gave out loans with higher loan-to-income ratios, were more likely to securitize the loans, and had higher delinquency rates ex-post.

By linking lobbying and campaign contribution data with actual voting and lending behavior, Igan presents evidence that suggests that lobbying by the financial sector influences legislators' voting behavior. Moreover, the financial institutions that benefit the most from deregulation—such as subprime lenders—are more likely to devote greater resources to lobbying activity.

Another prominent topic in political economy is income inequality (see Piketty 2014, as well as the papers in the summer 2013 issue of the *Journal of Economic Perspectives*). Politics, in turn, can exacerbate income inequality if the political process overweights those with high incomes. Larry Bartels (2009) filed the opening claim that members of Congress represented the views of their rich constituents and largely ignored the views of poor ones. Bartels's methodological and measurement groups have subsequently been challenged (Bhatti and Erikson 2011; Brunner, Ross, and Washington 2013).

Tausanovitch brings big data to this problem by making substantial increases in the number of respondents used in the analysis. He estimates an item response model for 362,000 respondents. The large sample size permits analysis of the U.S. House of Representatives, whereas the earlier studies were limited to the Senate. Doing so required developing special software that took advantage of graphical processing units in desktop computers. The paper innovates in a way that goes beyond increasing sample size. Whereas Bartels and Erikson and Bhatti used responses to a single survey item, five-point or seven-point ideological self-placements, Tausanovitch applies the item response model to policy questions. He can then measure ideology on a continuum and eliminate the granularity in the other measurements. For a similar policy question approach but with smaller samples, see Stephen Jessee (2012).

The bottom line in the results is that how the distribution of income in a district influences whether Democrats or Republicans represent the district is far more important than how differences in income affect within-party representation. Moreover, the mean overall preference of the district, which is likely to have less measurement error than either the mean preference of the poor or the mean preference of the rich, is a better predictor than the mean of either group.

One limitation of the Tausanovitch study is that income is top-coded so that the "rich" in the study are all respondents reporting an income over $100,000—hardly the infamous 1 percent (Edsall 2013). One could apply the big data capacity of the Bonica study to use contributor zip codes to compute a money-weighted average ideology of contributors in a district. This might be a better measurement of the opinion of the truly rich, and it could be run through the Tausanovitch analytics.

Rather than looking at contributions, roll call voting, public opinion, or cheap talk text, the paper by Sharyn O'Halloran, Sameer Maskey, Geraldine McAllister, David K. Park, and Kaiping Chen goes directly to a policy analysis of financial regulatory structure. A major objective, shared with the Bonica and Dimmery and Peterson papers, is to replace tedious hand-coding of volumes of text with automated procedures. And volumes there are— the paper ambitiously tackles all regulatory legislation since 1950. The analytical problem has worsened over time as legislation has become increasingly wordy. (Dodd-Frank alone has over 30,000 words.) The main topics of interest, classic in the political science literature, are regulatory delegation and procedural constraints. The work shows that traditional coding and automated coding are complementary.

The authors use their processing of text to test two hypotheses: (1) that there is more discretion when the president and Congress have similar preferences or there is more market uncertainty, and (2) that higher risk aversion leads to more regulation, but with more discretion.

To summarize the methodology, O'Halloran and her coauthors started by identifying the texts of all financial regulation laws to the exclusion of those dealing with mortgage lending. The laws were then coded for delegation and procedural constraint. Both delegation and constraint were reduced to one-dimensional indexes, and discretion was measured as the product of the delegation index and one minus the constraint index. The analysis shows that discretion is least with a Democratic president and a Republican Congress.

REFERENCES

Albertson, Bethany, and Shana Gadarian. 2014. "Was the Facebook Emotion Experiment Unethical?" *Washington Post,* July 1.

Baker, Scott. 2014. "Debt and the Consumption Response to Household Income Shocks." April. http://web.stanford.edu/~srbaker/Papers/Baker_DebtConsumption.pdf (accessed May 31, 2016).

Barberá, Pablo. 2015. "Birds of the Same Feather Tweet Together: Bayesian Ideal Point Estimation Using Twitter Data." *Political Analysis* 23(1): 76–91.

Bartels, Larry M. 2009. *Unequal Democracy: The Political Economy of the New Gilded Age.* Princeton, N.J.: Princeton University Press.

Bhatti, Yosef, and Robert S. Erikson. 2011. "How Poorly Are the Poor Represented in the U.S. Senate?" In *Who Gets Represented?* edited by Peter K. Enns and Christopher Wlezien (New York: Russell Sage Foundation).

Bonica, Adam. 2013. "Ideology and Interests in the Political Marketplace." *American Journal of Political Science* 57(2): 294–311.

———. 2014. "Mapping the Ideological Marketplace." *American Journal of Political Science* 58(2): 367–86.

———. 2016. "A Data-Driven Voter Guide for U.S. Elections: Adapting Quantitative Measures of the Preferences and Priorities of Political Elites to Help Voters Learn About Candidates." *RSF: The Russell Sage Foundation Journal of the Social Sciences* 2(7). doi: 10.7758/RSF.2016.2.7.02.

Bonica, Adam, Adam S. Chilton, and Maya Sen. 2015. "The Political Ideologies of American Lawyers." *Journal of Legal Analysis.* First published online October 13. doi: 10.1093/jla/lav011.

Bonica, Adam, David J. Rothman, and Howard L. Rosenthal. 2014. "The Political Polarization of Physicians in the United States: An Analysis of Campaign Contributions to Federal Elections, 1991–2012." *JAMA Internal Medicine* 174(8): 1308–17.

———. 2015. "The Political Alignment of U.S. Physicians: An Update Including Campaign Contributions to the Congressional Midterm Elections in 2014." *JAMA Internal Medicine* 175(7): 1236–37.

Brunner, Eric, Stephen L. Ross, and Ebonya Washington. 2013. "Does Less Income Mean Less Representation?" *American Economic Journal: Economic Policy* 5(2): 53–76.

Chae, David H., Sean Clouston, Mark L. Hatzenbuehler, Michael R. Kramer, Hannah L. F. Cooper, Sacoby M. Wilson, Seth I. Stephens-Davidowitz, Robert S. Gold, and Bruce G. Link. 2015. "Association Between an Internet-Based Measure of Area Racism and Black Mortality." *PLOS ONE* (April 24).

Dimmery, Drew, and Andrew Peterson. 2016. "Shining the Light on Dark Money: Political Spending by Nonprofits." *RSF: The Russell Sage Foundation Journal of the Social Sciences* 2(7). doi: 10.7758/RSF.2016.2.7.04.

Dobbie, Will, and Jae Song. 2015. "Debt Relief and Debtor Outcomes: Measuring the Effects of Consumer Bankruptcy Protection." *American Economic Review* 105(3): 1272–1311.

Edsall, Thomas B. 2013. "When Class Trumps Identity." *New York Times,* October 29. http://www.nytimes.com/2013/10/29/opinion/edsall-when-class-trumps-identity.html (accessed May 23, 2016).

Erikson, Robert S., and Thomas R. Palfrey. 2000. "Equilibria in Campaign Spending Games: Theory and Data." *American Political Science Review* 94(3): 595–609.

Gentzkow, Matthew, and Jesse M. Shapiro. 2010. "What Drives Media Slant? Evidence from U.S. Newspapers." *Econometrica* 78(1): 35–71.

Giannetti, Daniela. 2010. "Secret Voting in the Italian Parliament." Paper presented at the annual meeting of Rationalité et Sciences Sociales. College de France, Paris (June 3–4).

Griffin, John M., and Gonzalo Maturana. 2013. "Who Facilitated Misreporting in Securitized Loans?" Working paper. University of Texas, Austin.

Hersh, E. D., and M. Goldenberg. 2016. "Political Spillover Effects on Physician Clinical Practice." Working paper. Yale University, New Haven, Conn.

Igan, Deniz. 2016. "Home Truths: Promises and Challenges in Linking Mortgages and Political Influence." *RSF: The Russell Sage Foundation Journal of the Social Sciences* 2(7). doi: 10.7758/RSF.2016.2.7.05.

Imai, Kosuke, James Lo, and Jonathan Olmsted. 2015. "Fast Estimation of Ideal Points with Massive Data." Working paper. Princeton University.

Jessee, Stephen A. 2012. *Ideology and Spatial Voting*

in American Elections. New York: Cambridge University Press.

Keys, Benjamin J., Amit Seru, and Vikrant Vig. 2012. "Lender Screening and the Role of Securitization: Evidence from Prime and Subprime Mortgage Markets." *Review of Financial Studies* 25(7): 2071–108.

Kim, In Song. 2014. "Intra-industry Trade and Trade Liberalization: Evidence from Dyad-Level Tariff Data." Working paper. Massachusetts Institute of Technology, Cambridge.

Levitt, Steven D. 1994. "Using Repeat Challengers to Estimate the Effect of Campaign Spending on Election Outcomes in the U.S. House." *Journal of Political Economy* 102(4): 777–98.

Lewis, Jeffrey B., and Chris Tausanovitch. 2015. "When Does Joint Scaling Allow for Direct Comparisons of Preferences?" Working paper. University of California, Los Angeles.

Lucca, David, Amit Seru, and Francesco Trebbi. 2014. "The Revolving Door and Worker Flows in Banking Regulation." *Journal of Monetary Economics* 65: 17–32.

McCarty, Nolan, Keith T. Poole, and Howard Rosenthal. 2006. *Polarized America: The Dance of Ideology and Unequal Riches.* Cambridge, Mass.: MIT Press.

Mian, Atif, and Amir Sufi. 2014. *House of Debt: How They (and You) Caused the Great Recession, and How We Can Prevent It from Happening Again.* Chicago: University of Chicago Press.

———. 2015. "Fraudulent Income Overstatement on Mortgage Applications During the Credit Expansion of 2002 to 2005." Working paper. Princeton University and University of Chicago.

Mian, Atif, Kamalesh Rao, and Amir Sufi. 2013. "Household Balance Sheets, Consumption, and the Economic Slump." *Quarterly Journal of Economics* (July 25). doi: 10.1093/qje/qjt020.

Mian, Atif, Amir Sufi, and Nasim Khoshkhou. 2016. "Government Economic Policy, Sentiments and Consumption." *NBER* working paper.

Mian, Atif R., Amir Sufi, and Francesco Trebbi. 2010. "The Political Economy of the U.S. Mortgage Default Crisis," *American Economic Review* 100(5): 1967–98.

O'Halloran, Sharyn, Sameer Maskey, Geraldine McAllister, David K. Park, and Kaiping Chen. 2016. "Data Science and Political Economy: Application to Financial Regulatory Structure." *RSF: The Russell Sage Foundation Journal of the Social Sciences* 2(7). doi: 10.7758/RSF.2017.2.6.06.

Piketty, Thomas. 2014. *Capital in the Twenty-First Century.* Cambridge, Mass.: Belknap Press of Harvard University Press.

Piketty, Thomas, and Emmanuel Saez. 2003. "Income Inequality in the United States, 1913–1998. *Quarterly Journal of Economics* 118(1): 1–39.

Poole, Keith T., and Howard L. Rosenthal. 1991. "Patterns of Congressional Voting." *American Journal of Political Science* 35(1): 228–78.

———. 2007. *Ideology and Congress.* New Brunswick, N.J.: Transaction Publishers.

Shor, Boris, and Nolan McCarty. 2011. "The Ideological Mapping of American Legislatures." *American Political Science Review* 105(3): 530–51.

Tausanovitch, Chris. 2016. "Income, Ideology, and Representation." *RSF: The Russell Sage Foundation Journal of the Social Sciences* 2(7). doi: 10.7758/RSF.2016.2.7.03.

Wolfinger, Raymond E., and Steven J. Rosenstone. 1980. *Who Votes?* New Haven, Conn.: Yale University Press.

A Data-Driven Voter Guide for U.S. Elections: Adapting Quantitative Measures of the Preferences and Priorities of Political Elites to Help Voters Learn About Candidates

ADAM BONICA

Internet-based voter advice applications have experienced tremendous growth across Europe in recent years but have yet to be widely adopted in the United States. By comparison, the candidate-centered U.S. electoral system, which routinely requires voters to consider dozens of candidates across a dizzying array of local, state, and federal offices each time they cast a ballot, introduces challenges of scale to the systematic provision of information. Only recently have methodological advances combined with the rapid growth in publicly available data on candidates and their supporters to bring a comprehensive data-driven voter guide within reach. This paper introduces a set of newly developed software tools for collecting, disambiguating, and merging large amounts of data on candidates and other political elites. It then demonstrates how statistical methods developed by political scientists to measure the preferences and expressed priorities of politicians can be adapted to help voters learn about candidates.

Keywords: ideal point estimation, text-as-data, supervised machine learning, voting advice applications

The onset and proliferation of web applications that help voters identify the party that best represents their policy preferences, commonly known as "voter advice applications," is among the most exciting recent developments in the practice and study of electoral politics (Alvarez et al. 2014; Louwerse and Rosema 2013; Rosema, Anderson, and Walgrave 2014). After their emergence in the early 2000s, they quickly spread throughout Europe and beyond and have since become increasingly popular among voters. In recent elections in Germany, the Netherlands, and Switzerland, upwards of 30 to 40 percent of the electorates used these tools to vote (Ladner, Felder, and Fivaz 2010). Despite their growing popularity, voter advice applications have yet to make significant headway in the United States. While voter advice applications have excelled in parliamentary democracies, which require data on the issue positions for a small number of parties, the multi-tiered, candidate-centered U.S. electoral system introduces challenges of size, scale, and complexity to the systematic provision of information.

Reformers have long advocated for greater disclosure and government transparency as a means to inform voters and enhance electoral accountability. In justifying the value of disclosure in *Buckley v. Valeo*, the Supreme Court wrote that "disclosure provides the electorate with information 'as to where political campaign money comes from and how it is spent by the candidate' in order to aid the voters in evaluating those who seek federal office. It allows voters to place each candidate in the political spectrum more precisely than is often

---

Adam Bonica is assistant professor of political science at Stanford University. He is also co-founder at Crowdpac Inc.

Direct correspondence to: Adam Bonica at bonica@stanford.edu, Stanford University, Encina Hall West, Room 307, 616 Serra St., Stanford, CA 94305-6044.

possible solely on the basis of party labels and campaign speeches."[1] Disclosure requirements have long been a central component of campaign finance regulation, churning out millions upon millions of records each election cycle. Yet despite the stringent disclosure requirements and reporting standards, making data transparent and freely available is seldom sufficient on its own. More is needed to translate this raw information into a truly useful resource for voters.

Thus far, the use of data-intensive applications in U.S. politics has primarily been in service of parties and campaigns. This is perhaps best exemplified by the Obama campaign's success in leveraging large-scale databases to learn about voters and predict their behavior, which was widely lauded following the 2012 elections (Issenberg 2012). However, the true potential of the data revolution in U.S. politics might very well be realized by harnessing its power to help voters, donors, and other consumers of politics learn about candidates. As political scientists are well aware, the information available on political elites—through what they say, how they vote, and how they network and fund-raise—is much richer and of higher quality than the information available on the mass public. Delivering on the promise of disclosure requires (1) a means of summarizing the information contained in the raw data into a format that is more easily interpreted but still highly informative, and (2) an intuitive platform for accessing data quickly and efficiently. The first is a familiar problem to social scientists, who have spent decades developing numerous data reduction methods to summarize revealed preference data. Only more recently has the possibility of developing a platform to enable voters to interact with the data come within reach.

This paper introduces a new database and modeling framework developed to power Crowdpac's new political information platform (Willis 2014). I begin with a discussion of how methods developed by political scientists to measure the policy preferences and expressed priorities of politicians can be adapted to help voters learn about candidates. For many of the same reasons they have proven useful to political scientists, there could be significant value in retooling these quantitative measures of political preferences for a wider audience. After providing an overview of the automated data collection and entity resolution techniques used to build and maintain the database, I introduce a modeling framework developed to generate issue-specific measures of policy preferences incorporating established methods for analyzing political text, voting records, and campaign contributions.

DEMOCRATIZING POLITICAL DATA

The U.S. electoral system imposes considerable informational costs on voters. Even for the most sophisticated of voters, filling out a ballot is a daunting task. Depending on the state, a typical ballot might ask voters to select candidates in dozens of races and decide on multiple ballot measures. The informational costs are particularly high in primary elections and other contests where voters are unable to rely on partisan cues and other informational shortcuts and find themselves unsure about which candidate is best aligned with their preferences.

Information is crucial to effective political participation. In the context of elections, an informed vote is a matter of being confident in a set of predictions about how the candidates under consideration would behave in office. The uncertainty experienced by voters in the polling booth can arise from many sources, but much of it is a consequence of information asymmetries rather than the capriciousness of politicians. Most politicians have well-defined policy preferences but often lack either the means or incentives to communicate them clearly to voters. Politicians rarely behave unpredictably when presented with familiar choices.

Even though disclosure data has been sold as providing a service to voters, those best positioned to utilize it have been campaigns, lobbyists, and special-interest groups. This is reflected in the market for political information. The most sophisticated data collection and analytics have gone into subscription fee–based services (such as Legistorm and Catalist) and

---

1. *Buckley v. Valeo* 96 S. Ct. 612; 46 L. Ed. 2d 659; 1976 U.S. LEXIS 16; 76-1 U.S. Tax Cas. (CCH) P9189.2.

are targeted at these groups. Insider knowledge about which politicians are power brokers, which races are likely to be competitive, and where to direct contributions is a service that lobbyists provide to high-powered clients.

Past efforts to build a comprehensive political information platform for voters in U.S. elections have all struggled with the problem of conveying meaningful signals about the policy preferences of non-incumbents and officeholders beyond a select group of legislative bodies. In the 1990s, Project Vote Smart adopted an innovative strategy for dealing with this asymmetry with respect to incumbency status. The National Political Awareness Test (NPAT) was a major effort to compile policy positions by surveying candidates. Unfortunately, after a decline in response rates, due in part to active discouragement by party leaders, NPAT achieved only limited success. Project Vote Smart has since shifted strategies and begun to code issue positions manually, based on candidates' public statements. This approach has shown some promise but is limited by issues of scalability, completeness, and coder reliability.

There are three main challenges in creating such a resource for the public: (1) automating the collection and maintenance of a large-scale database drawn from numerous sources; (2) devising effective ways to summarize and visualize data on candidates; and (3) designing a user interface that is easy to understand and follow for those with varying levels of political sophistication. This paper introduces a set of data-driven strategies to address these challenges.

DATA ARCHITECTURE

This section introduces the new database that serves as a central repository for data on candidates and political elites. The database draws on three main sources of data: political text, voting and legislative behavior, and campaign contributions.

A system of automated scrapers is used to collect and process new data as they become available. To ensure scalability, a new data source is not included until the feasibility of maintaining it with minimal human supervision has been established. Beyond automating the compiling and updating of the database, transforming the raw data into a usable format presented its own challenges. In particular, a solution was needed for merging and disambiguating data drawn from difference sources. This was managed with customized automated identity resolution and record-linkage algorithms supplemented by strategic use of human-assisted coding when identifying personal contributions made by candidates. Each of the three data sources is described in this section.

Political Text

Political text is any written or transcribed public statement by a political actor. In its current state, the database of text largely comprises documents originating from legislation and the *Congressional Record*, which contains transcripts of all proceedings, floor debates, and extensions of remarks in Congress. Congressional bill text is taken from Congress.gov. Additional contextual data on legislation, such as information on sponsorship, co-sponsorship, and committee activity, are also collected. Importantly, the Congressional Research Service (CRS) provides subject codes for each bill. These tags are used to train the topic model discussed later. The *Congressional Record* is taken from the Federal Digital System (FDsys) of the U.S. Government Printing Office (GPO). Each document in the database is linked to a candidate ID and, when applicable, a bill ID. Bill authorship is attributed to the sponsor(s). Speeches made during floor debates are attributed to the speaker and, when applicable, any bills specifically referenced during the speech. The text database currently includes over half a million documents.

Legislative Voting

Congressional voting records are downloaded from voteview.com via the W-NOMINATE R package (Poole et al. 2011). Bills and amendments are assigned unique identifiers that provide a crosswalk to other tables in the database.

Campaign Contributions

Contribution records are drawn from an augmented version of the Database on Ideology,

Figure 1. Data Architecture of Database on Ideology, Money, and Elections (DIME)

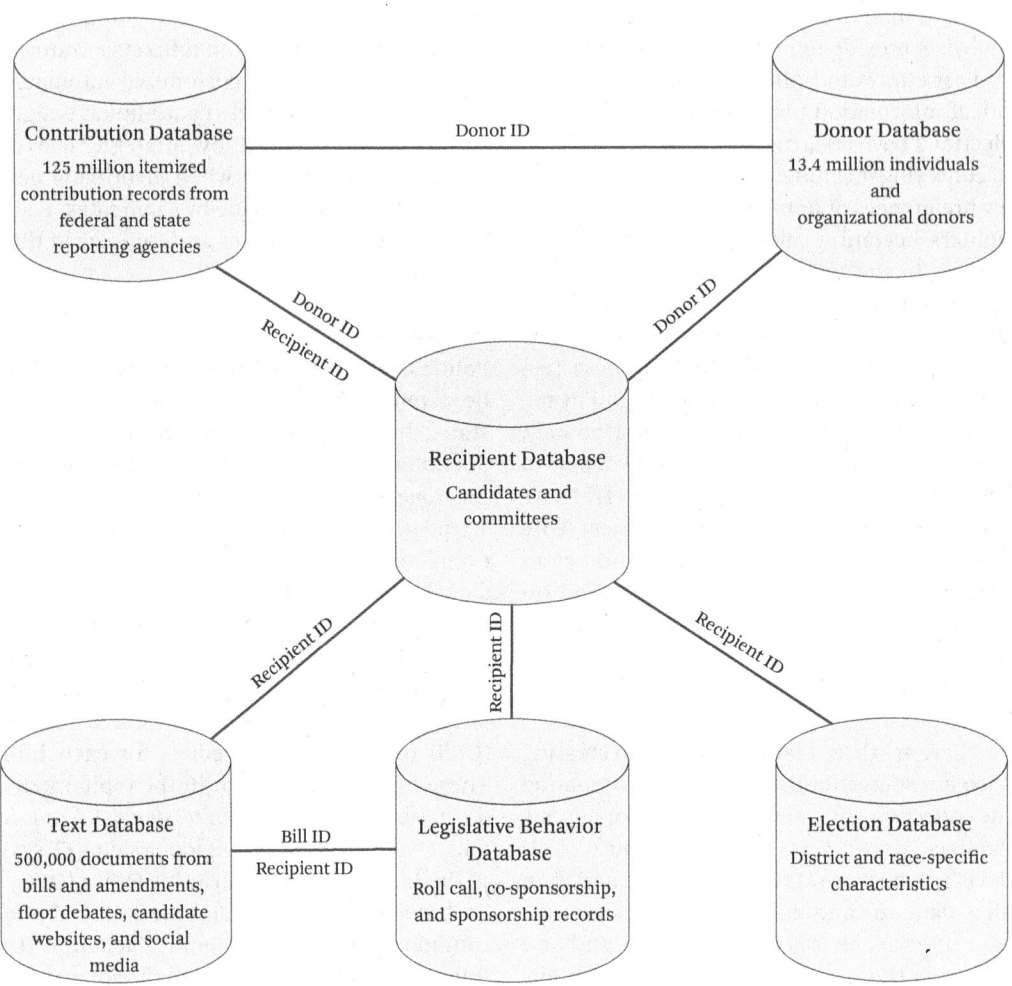

Source: Author's calculations.

Money, and Elections (DIME) (Bonica 2014).[2] Since nearly every serious candidate for state or federal office engages in fund-raising (either as a recipient or a donor), campaign finance data provide the scaffolding for constructing the recipient database. Figure 1 presents a visual representation of the data architecture. The database consists of six tables corresponding to the different record types. The unique identifiers for candidates, donors, and bills serve as crosswalks between the tables. Each line in the figure indicate a crosswalk between two tables.

The recipient table plays a central role in structuring the data. It can be mapped onto each of the other databases by one or more crosswalks. It contains variables for numerous characteristics, including the office sought, bi-

---

2. For information on access to the database and reference documentation, see Adam Bonica, Database on Ideology, Money in Politics, and Elections (DIME): public version 1.0 (computer file) (Stanford, Calif.: Stanford University Libraries, 2013), http://data.stanford.edu/dime (accessed May 31, 2016).

ographical profiles, past campaigns and offices held, fund-raising statistics (for example, totals by source or amounts raised from donors within the district), committee assignments, and various other data rendered on the site. Each row represents a candidate-cycle observation. The recipient table currently includes 360,173 rows extending back to 1979, covering 105,967 distinct candidates and 38,689 political committees. Additional identity resolution processing is applied to candidates who have run for state and federal office to ensure that each one is linked to a single identifier.

The contribution table contains records of more than 125 million itemized contributions to state and federal elections. Each record maps onto the recipient database via the corresponding recipient ID. Contribution records can also be linked to the originating candidate or committee for the set of recipients who have donated via the contributor IDs. The donor table summarizes and standardizes the information in the contribution database into a more usable format with a single row per donor.

The text table includes documents scraped from legislative text for bills and amendments, floor speeches, candidate web pages, and social media accounts. Every document is linked to either a candidate from the recipient table or a bill or amendment from the legislative table—or both in the case of sponsored legislation.

By combining these data sources, a single database query can return a wealth of information on a candidate, including information on the candidate's ideology, fund-raising activity, and donors, his or her personal donation history, sponsored and co-sponsored legislation, written and spoken text, voting records, electoral history, personal and political biographies, and more. All of the data sources needed to replicate the database schema are available for download as part of DIME or as part of a supplemental database of legislative text and votes titled DIME+.[3]

The remaining sections explain the modeling framework applied to the database.

OVERALL MEASURES OF CANDIDATE IDEOLOGY

Beginning in the late 1970s, political scientists began combining techniques from econometrics and psychometrics to study the preferences of political elites (Aldrich and McKelvey 1977; Poole and Rosenthal 1985). This pioneering work found that low-dimensional mapping is highly predictive of congressional roll call voting. With the exception of a few periods in American history, a single dimension explains the lion's share of congressional voting outcomes (Poole and Rosenthal 1997). Ideal point estimation methods have since been used to measure the preferences of political actors serving in institutions other than Congress, including the courts (Epstein et al. 2007; Martin and Quinn 2002) and state legislatures (Shor and McCarty 2011).

The various applications have revealed elite preferences to be low-dimensional across a wide range of political institutions and demonstrated that positions along a liberal-conservative dimension are informative signals about policy preferences. However, relying on voting records to measure preferences precludes generating ideal points for nonincumbent candidates and most nonlegislative office-holders.

A particular challenge has been in comparing ideal points of actors across voting institutions (Bailey 2007; Shor and McCarty 2011). In recent years, political scientists have developed methods to measure preferences from various other sources of data, including candidate surveys (Ansolabehere, Snyder, and Stewart 2001; Burden 2004), campaign contributions (McCarty and Poole 1998), political text (Laver, Benoit, and Garry 2003; Monroe and Maeda 2004; Monroe, Colaresi, and Quinn 2008; Slapin and Proksch 2008), co-sponsorship networks (Peress 2013), voter evaluations (Hare et al. 2014), and Twitter follower networks (Barberá 2015).

The model used here to generate scores for candidates overcomes this problem by scaling campaign contributions using the common-

---

3. See note 2. The supplemental legislative database is hosted on Harvard Dataverse at http://dx.doi.org/10.7910/DVN/BO7WOW (accessed May 31, 2016).

space DIME methodology (Bonica 2014). The key advantages of this approach are its inclusiveness and scalability. The vast interconnected flows of campaign dollars tie American politics together. The resulting data make it possible to track a broad range of candidates, including non-incumbent candidates who have not previously held elected office, and to reach much further down the ballot. The data also provide estimates of how liberal or conservative individual donors are and place them in a common space with other candidates and organizations spanning local, state, and federal politics.

Campaign Finance Measures
Ideal point estimates for donors and candidates are recovered from campaign finance data using the common-space DIME methodology (Bonica 2014). I refer to Bonica (2014) for a complete treatment of the methodology. Here I provide a general overview of the measurement strategy and validation.

The measurement strategy is relatively straightforward. It relies on donors' collective assessments of candidates as revealed by their contribution patterns. The core assumption is that donors prefer candidates who share their policy views to those who do not. As a result, contributors are assumed—at least in part—to distribute funds in accordance with their evaluations of candidate ideology. As a result, by researching and seeking out candidates who share their policy preferences, donors provide information about the preferences of candidates.

Bonica (2014) offers three main pieces of evidence to validate the measures. First, the DIME scores are strongly correlated with vote-based measures of ideology such as DW-NOMINATE scores, providing strong evidence of their external validity. Second, there is a strong correspondence between contributor and recipient scores for candidates who have both fund-raised and made donations to other candidates, indicating that independently estimated sets of ideal points reveal similar information about an individual's ideology. For the 1,638 federal candidates who ran in the 2014 congressional elections and have scores as both donors and recipients, the correlations between contributor and recipient ideal points are $\rho = 0.97$ overall, $\rho = 0.92$ among Democrats, and $\rho = 0.94$ among Republicans. Third, the scores for individual donors and recipients are robust to controlling for candidate characteristics related to theories of strategic giving, such as incumbency status and electoral competitiveness.

An important claim made here is that the fund-raising activities of non-incumbents are predictive of how they will behave if elected to office. One way to assess the non-incumbent estimates is to compare scores recovered for successful challenger and open-seat candidates with their future scores as incumbents. The correlations between non-incumbent and incumbent CFscores is $r = 0.96$ overall, $r = 0.93$ for Republicans, and $r = 0.88$ for Democrats. This is consistent across candidates for state and federal office (Bonica 2014).

In order for the model to estimate a score for a candidate, the candidate must have received contributions from at least two distinct donors who also gave to at least one other candidate. This covers the vast majority of candidates running for state and federal offices. The model also assigns scores to all donors who contributed to at least two candidates. The donor scores are estimated independently of the recipient scores and exclude any contributions made to one's own campaign.

Roll Call Measures
Roll call measures are estimated for candidates who have served in Congress using optimal classification (OC) (Poole 2000). OC is a nonparametric unfolding procedure built directly on the geometry of spatial voting. The scores are from the first dimension of a two-dimensional joint scaling of the House and the Senate based on votes cast during the 108th to 113th Congresses. The roll call–based measures are nearly identical to the common-space DW-NOMINATE scores.

Combining Information Across Measures
Measures derived from distinct data sources may differ in the extent to which they condition on certain areas of politics and types of concerns. For example, Congress rarely votes on socially charged issues such as abortion and same-sex marriage. Yet such issues often fea-

Figure 2. Comparison of Scores for Candidate Ideology Generated from Different Data Sources

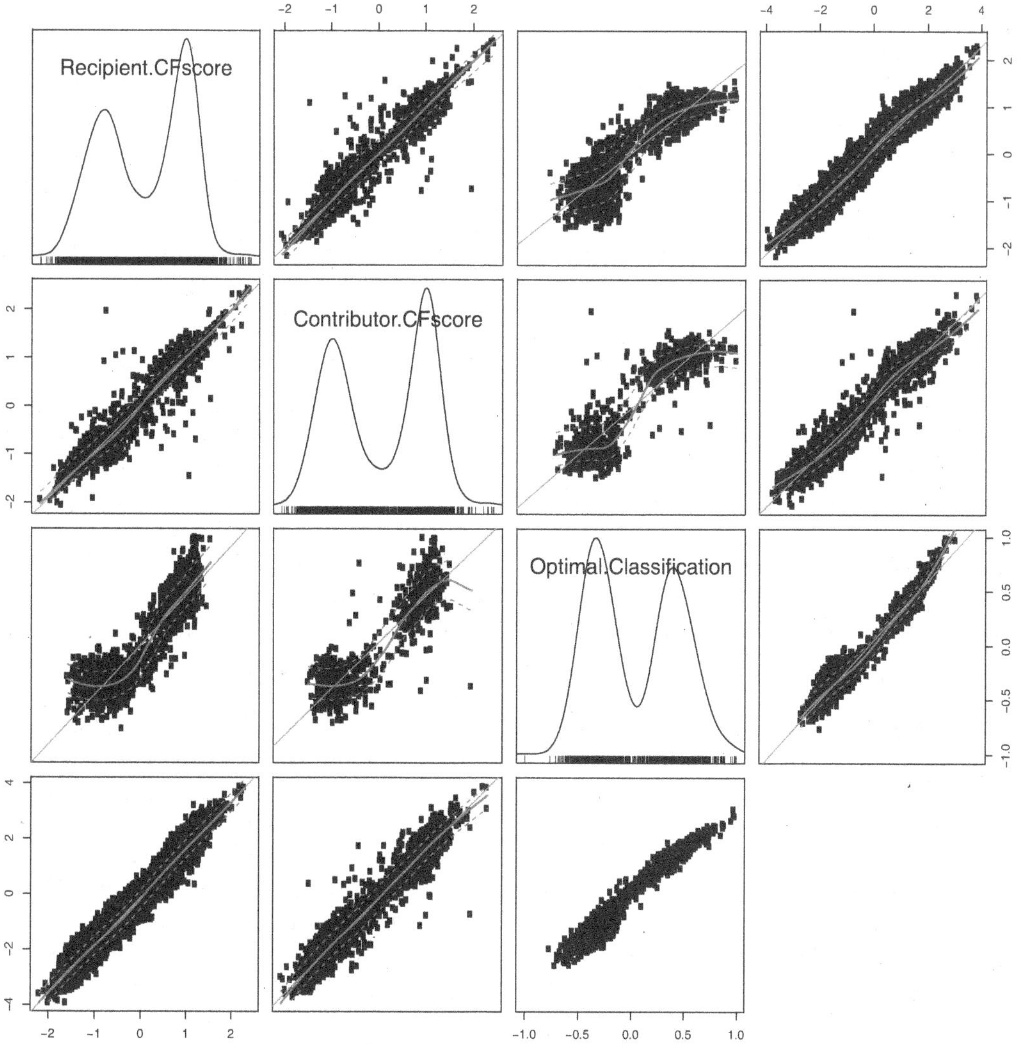

Source: Author's calculations.

ture prominently in campaign rhetoric and are a frequent subject of ballot initiatives. PACs and ballot committees that focus on these issues consistently draw large numbers of donors. This suggests value in combining information across measures.

Given the availability of multiple measures of candidate ideology, I average information across different sets of scores. I utilize a multiple over-imputation framework designed to handle multiple continuous variables with measurement error and missing data (Blackwell, Honaker, and King 2010). After imputing five sets of scores, I run a separate principle component analysis (PCA) on each data set. The overall scores are calculated by averaging over candidate scores from the first dimension recovered in each of the runs.

Figure 2 provides a comparison of scores generated from different data sources and the averaged scores. Given that the sets of scores are highly correlated, the first PCA dimension explains most of the variance. The averaged scores correlate with the recipient scores at $\rho = 0.98$, the contributor scores at $\rho = 0.96$, and the roll call scores at $\rho = 0.98$.

A MODEL TO MEASURE CANDIDATE PRIORITIES AND POSITIONS ACROSS ISSUES

Scoring candidates along a single dimension provides highly informative summaries of their policy preferences. Many voters and donors might also be interested in seeing how the preferences and expressed priorities of candidates vary by issue. The following sections outline a three-stage modeling strategy for measuring preferences and expressed priorities across issue dimensions that combines topic modeling, ideal point estimation, and machine learning methods. The first stage applies a topic model to the database of political text. The second stage estimates issue-specific ideal points for legislators based on past voting records using the estimated topic weights to identify the dimensionality of roll calls. The third stage trains a support-vector machine to predict issue scores for a wider set of candidates by conditioning on shared sources of data.

A Topic Model for Political Text

Topic models in their various forms have been extensively used in the study of politics (Grimmer 2010; Grimmer and Stewart 2013; Lauderdale and Clark 2014; Roberts et al. 2014). Political text is particularly well suited to the task of categorizing documents by issue area, whether it be bills, press releases, public speeches, or debates. Topic models offer a computational approach to automating the process of organizing large corpuses of documents into a set of issue categories. This is accomplished by breaking down each document into a set of words or phrases (n-grams) that then can be analyzed as text-as-data. The relative word frequencies found in each document contain information about which documents are most closely associated with which topics. In cases where the set of topics is reasonably well understood prior to the analysis, as is the case here, supervised methods can be used. These methods typically rely on a sample of human-coded documents to train a model that can then be used to infer topics for other documents.

The type of topic model used here is a partially labeled dirichlet allocation (PLDA) model (Ramage, Manning, and Dumais 2011). The PLDA model is a partially supervised topic model designed for use with corpuses where topic labels are assigned to documents in an unstructured or incomplete manner. An important feature of the model is that it allows for documents that address multiple or overlapping issue areas to be tagged with more than one topic. In addition to the specified issue categories, the model allows for a latent category that acts as a catchall or background category.

Issue Labels

The model makes use of issue labels assigned by the Congressional Research Service as a starting point in training the PLDA model. For each bill introduced, the CRS assigns one or more labels from a wide range of potential categories. Although the CRS labels have the advantage of being specific to the task at hand, they are neither well structured nor assigned based on a systematic coding scheme. The raw data include a total of 4,386 issue codes, and it is not uncommon for coders to tag a bill with a dozen or more labels. Many of these issue codes are overly idiosyncratic (for example, "dyslexia" and "grapes"), closely related or overlapping ("oil and gas," "oil-well drilling," "natural gas," "gasoline," and "oil shales"), or subcategorizations. To streamline the issue labels, a secondary layer of normalization is applied on top of the CRS issue codes. This is done by mapping issue labels onto a more general set of categories. CRS issue labels that overlap two larger categories are tagged accordingly (for example, "minority employment" ⇒ "civil rights" and "jobs and the economy"). CRS issue labels that are either too idiosyncratic (for example, "noise pollution") or too ambiguous (for example, "competition") to cleanly map onto a category are removed. All other documents, including those scraped from social media feeds and candidate websites, are used only during the inference stage.

Constructing the Training Set

The training set consists of all documents that can be linked to legislation with CRS issue tags. Since the CRS issue tags are derived from the content of the legislation, bills are especially important during the training stage. Documents that contain floor speeches made in relation to a specific bill, usually as part of the floor debate, are also included as part of the training set. Such inclusion assumes that the CRS categories assigned to a bill also apply to its floor debate. As such, topic loadings for a bill can reflect both its official language and the floor speeches of members during debate. This is intended as a way to capture how legislators (both supporters and opponents) speak about a bill and better grasp the types of concerns raised during debate. For example, the official language of a health care bill might mostly speak to policy related to health care, but often a single paragraph or specific provision amounting to a small fraction of the bill's language (for example, a provision relating to abortion or reproductive rights) is seized on and becomes the focus of the floor debate. The coding scheme should take this into account by giving more weight to the types of issues that legislators emphasize when speaking about the bill.

Linking Documents to Bills and Legislators

Floor speeches transcribed in the *Congressional Record* are organized into documents based on the identity of the speaker and, if applicable, related legislation. A customized parser was used to extract the speaker's identity, filter on the relevant body of text, and link floor speeches to bill numbers. In order for a document to be linked to a bill, the bill number must be included somewhere in the heading or the speaker must directly reference the name or number of the legislation in the text. Not all floor speeches are related to specific legislation. Legislators are routinely given the opportunity to make commemorations or generally address an issue of their choosing. These speeches often are used as position-taking exercises and are thus informative signals about the legislator's expressed priorities.

PLDA Model and Results

The PLDA model was fit using the Stanford Topic Model Toolkit (Ramage et al. 2009). Terms were organized as both unigrams and bigrams.[4] In addition to the typical list of stopwords included in the Natural Language Took Kit (NLTK) Python package, several terms specific to congressional proceedings and legislation were removed from the text. Stemming was performed using the WordNet lemmatizer, again provided by the NTLK Python package. Rare terms found in fewer than one hundred documents were filtered out. Documents that did not meet the minimum threshold of ten terms were excluded. The model was iterated five thousand times to ensure convergence.

To give a sense of which words are associated with which topics, table 1 reports the top eight words identified by the model as being most closely associated with each topic.

In addition to estimating topic loadings for bills, it is possible to construct measures of the expressed issue priorities of candidates by combining the set of documents linked to an individual, including sponsored legislation. As a way to validate the expressed priorities of legislators, Justin Grimmer (2010) argues that leaders of congressional committees should allocate more attention to the issue topics under their jurisdiction. Figure 3 replicates an analysis found in Grimmer and Stewart (2013) that compares the average attention paid to each topic by Senate committee leaders to the average attention allocated by the rest of the Senate. Note that the analysis here differs in that it compares all members of House and Senate committees with jurisdiction over an issue, not just committee chairs and ranking members. The figure reveals that for every included category, the topic model results indicate that committee members devote significantly more attention to related issues.

Issue-Specific Optimal Classification

In this section, I introduce an issue-specific optimal classification scaling model. The OC scaling model is an attractive option for this application because of its computational efficiency, robustness to missing values, and ability to jointly scale members of the House and Senate in a common-space by using those who

---

4. A unigram is a single word in a document (for example, "taxes"), and a bigram is the combination of two consecutive words ("cut taxes").

Table 1. Top Terms by Issue Category

	term 1	term 2	term 3	term 4	term 5	term 6	term 7	term 8
Latent	work	make	congress	million	important	country	nation	going
Federal agencies and regulation	commission	sec	office	activity	requirement	director	government	development
Economy	tax	code	credit	revenue	taxable	respect	qualified	benefit
Health care	care	drug	medical	medicare	coverage	disease	patient	insurance
Education	school	education	grant	student	educational	child	local	eligible
Defense and foreign policy	country	government	international	foreign	war	world	force	right
Banking and finance	financial	loan	insurance	housing	credit	mortgage	business	company
Law courts and judges	court	action	person	product	violation	claim	civil	employee
Energy	energy	fuel	oil	gas	vehicle	renewable	facility	production
Procedural	fiscal	budget	appropriation	available	provided	authority	office	congress
Parks and recreation	land	area	management	forest	water	river	project	park
Environment	water	administrator	environmental	species	protection	system	control	project
Veterans' affairs	veteran	defense	military	force	armed	affair	operation	code
Crime	enforcement	child	crime	criminal	attorney	justice	general	grant
Agriculture	food	agricultural	agriculture	farm	producer	crop	payment	assistance
Transportation	transportation	project	safety	system	vehicle	highway	air	funding
Immigration	alien	immigration	border	homeland	status	employer	visa	nationality
Intelligence and surveillance	intelligence	general	internet	person	surveillance	electronic	foreign	privacy
Higher education	education	student	institution	college	higher	science	university	loan
Civil rights	election	right	candidate	vote	voting	voter	political	civil
Emergency	emergency	line	disaster	page	flood	SA	proposed	hurricane
Indian affairs	indian	tribe	native	tribal	land	water	agreement	hawaiian
Women's issues	woman	violence	sexual	assault	domestic	victim	child	prevention
Abortion and social conservatism	right	abortion	religious	cell	woman	human	stem	research
Guns	firearm	person	gun	general	attorney	model	code	ammunition

Source: Author's calculations.

Note: Topics are listed in descending order based on their relative weights. Bigrams are excluded from the table to enhance readability.

Figure 3. Average Attention to Topics by Senate Committee Leaders Compared to Average Attention by Other Senate Members

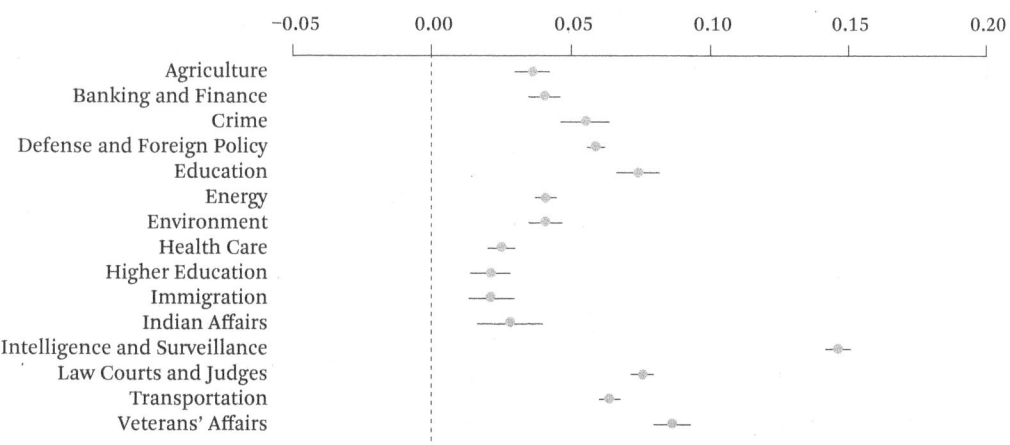

(Average Attention, Related Cmtes)−(Average Attention, Other MCs)

Source: Author's calculations.

served in both chambers as bridge observations (Poole 2000). The model follows recent methodological developments in multidimensional ideal point estimation (Clark and Lauderdale 2012; Gerrish and Blei 2012; Lauderdale and Clark 2014). Borrowing from the issue-adjusted ideal point model developed by Sean Gerrish and David Blei (2012), the dimensionality of roll calls is identified using a topic model trained on issue tags provided by the CRS. The issue-specific OC model differs in its approach to mapping the results from the topic model onto the dimensionality of roll calls. Gerrish and Blei incorporate a vector of issue adjustment parameters that in effect serve as dimension-specific utility shocks. The issue-specific OC model instead utilizes the basic geometry of spatial voting through the parameterization of the normal vectors. This approach distinguishes the issue-specific OC model from the approach taken by Tom Clark and Benjamin Lauderdale (2012), who similarly extend OC to generate issue-varying ideal points for U.S. Supreme Court justices by kernel-weighting errors based on substantive similarity. The approach is actually most similar to related work by Lauderdale and Clark (2014) that combines latent dirichlet allocation with an item response theory model.

In the standard OC model, the dimensionality of bill j is determined by a heuristic cutting plane algorithm that searches the parameter space for the normal vector N_j and corresponding cutting line c_j, which minimize classification errors. The issue-specific OC model instead differs by calculating the normal vectors based on the parameters recovered from the PLDA model. Given a k-length vector λ_j of topic weights for roll call j, the normal vector is calculated as $N_{jk} = \lambda_{jk}/\|\lambda_j\|$. Legislator ideal points are then projected onto the projection line: $w_i = \theta_i' N_j$. Given the mapping onto w, finding the optimal cutting point c_j is identical to a one-dimensional classification problem. Given the estimated roll call parameters, issue-specific ideal points can be recovered dimension by dimension. Holding parameters for $\theta_{i\text{-}k}$ constant, classification errors are minimized by finding the optimal value of θ_{ik} given c_j and the projected values $w_{ij} = \theta_{i\text{-}k}' N_{j\text{-}k} + \theta_{ik}' N_{jk}$. As an identification assumption, $\theta_{k=1}$ is fixed at its starting value.

A further extension to the OC model is the incorporation of kernel methods to capture the relative importance of bills to legislators. A member's sponsorship of a bill or contribution to the floor debate suggests that the bill has greater significance to her than other bills on which she is silent. The inputs to the kernel-weighting function are status as a sponsor or

Table 2. Roll Call Classification, 108th to 113th Congresses

	Correct Classification	Aggregate Proportional Reduction in Error	Errors	Weighted CC	Weighted APRE	Weighted Errors
One-dimensional OC	0.936	0.825	154569	0.938	0.818	179,598
Issue-specific OC	0.940	0.835	145430	0.943	0.832	166,126

Source: Author's calculations.

co-sponsor and the total word count devoted to the legislation. The weight matrix is constructed as follows:

$$\omega_{ij} = 1 + \gamma_1 sponsor_{ij} + \gamma_2 cosponsor_{ij} + \gamma_3 log(wordcount_{ij}) \quad (1)$$

The γ parameters are calibrated using a cross-validation scheme. Given a set of parameter values, the model is subjected to repeated runs with a fraction of observed vote choices held out. After the model run has converged, the total errors are calculated for a held-out sample based on the recovered estimates. Values are typically somewhere in the region of $\gamma_1 = 5$, $\gamma_2 = 2$, and $\gamma_3 = 1$.

Starting values are estimated separately for each dimension using a one-dimensional OC scaling with issue-weighted errors. Given an issue dimension k, errors on each roll call are weighted by the proportion of the related text associated with the issue. A classification error on a roll call where $\lambda_{jk} = 0.5$ is weighted 50 times that of an error on a roll call where $\lambda_{jk} = 0.01$. After dropping roll calls where $\lambda_{jk} < 0.01$, the model is run to convergence.

Table 2 reports the classification statistics for the issue-specific OC model. The issue-specific model increases correct classification (CC) over the one-dimensional model, but only marginally. Congressional voting has become so unidimensional that only a small fraction of voting behavior is left unexplained by a one-dimensional model. The issue-specific model explains a nontrivial percentage of the remaining error. However, this is slightly less than the reduction in error associated with adding a second dimension to the standard OC model.

The marginal increase in fit occurs largely by design and is explained by constraints built into the issue-specific OC model. Classifying roll call votes in multiple dimensions can be highly sensitive to slight changes to the position or angle of the cutting line. The cutting-plane search is free to precisely position the cutting line by simultaneously manipulating the normal vector and cutting line. Hard-coding the dimensionality of bills based on the topic loading constrains normal vectors and limits the search to c_j. These effects are further compounded by a modeling assumption, made largely in the interest of reducing computational costs, that constrains the values for $N_{jk} \geq 0$, corresponding to the vector of topic loadings for each bill from which they are calculated. This means that bill proposals must move policy on all relevant dimensions in the same direction (that is, toward the ideological left or right). For example, the model does not allow for a bill to move economic policy to the right but immigration policy to the left.[5]

To assess the extent to which holding the normal vectors fixed explains the marginal reduction in error, I ran the cutting-plane search algorithm with the legislator ideal points set at values recovered from the issue-specific model. Relaxing the constraint on the normal vectors resulted in an appreciable reduction in error: correct classification was boosted to 96.4 percent.

---

5. For a two-dimensional model, this would constrain the normal vector to the upper-right quadrant. This constraint could be relaxed by the addition of a sign vector, which would allow values in the normal vector to take on negative or positive values. For an in-depth discussion of this issue, see Lauderdale and Clark (2014).

Figures 4 and 5 display a series of parallel plots that compare ideal points from standard OC and issue-specific OC for members of the 108th and 113th Congresses. The points on the top are ideal points from a standard one-dimensional OC scaling. The points on the bottom are the corresponding issue-specific ideal points. The line segments trace changes in ideal points between models.

In contrast to the near-perfect separation between the parties in Congress in the one-dimensional OC model during the period under analysis, the issue-specific model does show increased partisan overlap for most issues. The issues for which this overlap is most apparent are abortion and social conservatism, agriculture, guns, immigration, Indian affairs, intelligence and surveillance, and women's issues.

Where the issue-specific model excels is in identifying key legislators who broke ranks on one or more issue dimensions. For example, the sole legislator to cross over on defense and foreign policy was Representative Jim Leach (R-IA), who was known for his progressive views on foreign affairs. Of the legislators to cross over on abortion and social conservatism, pro-life advocates Senator Ben Nelson (D-NE) and Representatives John Breaux (D-LA) and Bobby Bright (D-ALA) were the three most conservative Democrats, and pro-choice advocates Representatives Sherry Boehlert (R-NY) and Rob Simmons (R-CT) and Senator Olympia Snowe (R-ME) were the three most liberal Republicans. Although few legislators break with their party on any given issue dimension, the ones who do are often noteworthy and highly visible players on the issue who stand out as examples of either cross-pressured bipartisans or uncompromising hard-liners. Often the largest differences are associated with legislators who are active on an issue. On immigration, for example, the legislators whose issue-specific ideal points shifted them the most from their overall score were Senators Chuck Hagel (R-NE) and Jeff Flake (R-AZ), both of whom had co-sponsored bipartisan immigration reform bills at different points in time.

The issue-specific ideal points on the intelligence and surveillance dimension are especially revealing. Four of the most conservative Republicans—Representatives Ron Paul (R-TX) and Justin Amash (R-MI) and Senators Rand Paul (R-KY) and Mike Lee (R-UT)—voted so consistently against their party that they flipped to have some of the most liberal ideal points on the issue. This fits with the libertarian leanings of these candidates as well as their public and vocal opposition to government surveillance.

Changes in patterns of partisan overlap from the 108th Congress to the 113th can also be revealing. In the 108th, the issue-specific ideal points for a handful of Republicans, including Senators Lincoln Chafee (R-RI), George Voinovich (R-OH), Mike Dewine (R-OH), and John Warner (R-VA), accurately place them well to left of center on guns. By the 113th Congress, the only remaining Republican crossover was Senator Mark Kirk (R-IL), whereas the number of Democrats breaking with their party over gun policy had grown to include Senators Byron Dorgan (D-ND), Max Baucus (D-MT), and Mark Pryor (D-AR), Representatives Henry Cuellar (D-TX) and Kurt Schrader (D-TX), and several others.

Support Vector Regression

The final stage in the model integrates campaign contributions. The objective is to produce issue-specific ideal points for the vast majority of candidates who lack voting records. Ideally, the model would seamlessly integrate voting and contribution records to estimate issue-specific ideal points for the entire population of candidates simultaneously. Unfortunately, such an approach is out of reach. I instead rely on supervised machine learning methods.

The structure of campaign contributions has many similarities to text-as-data. The contingency matrix of donors and recipients is functionally similar to a document-term matrix, only with shorter documents and more highly informative words. As such, translating models originally designed for political text for use with campaign contributions is relatively straightforward. Although several classes of the models typically applied to textual analysis could be used here, I focus on support vector

Figure 4. Legislator Ideal Points from Classical OC and Issue-Specific OC (108th Congress)

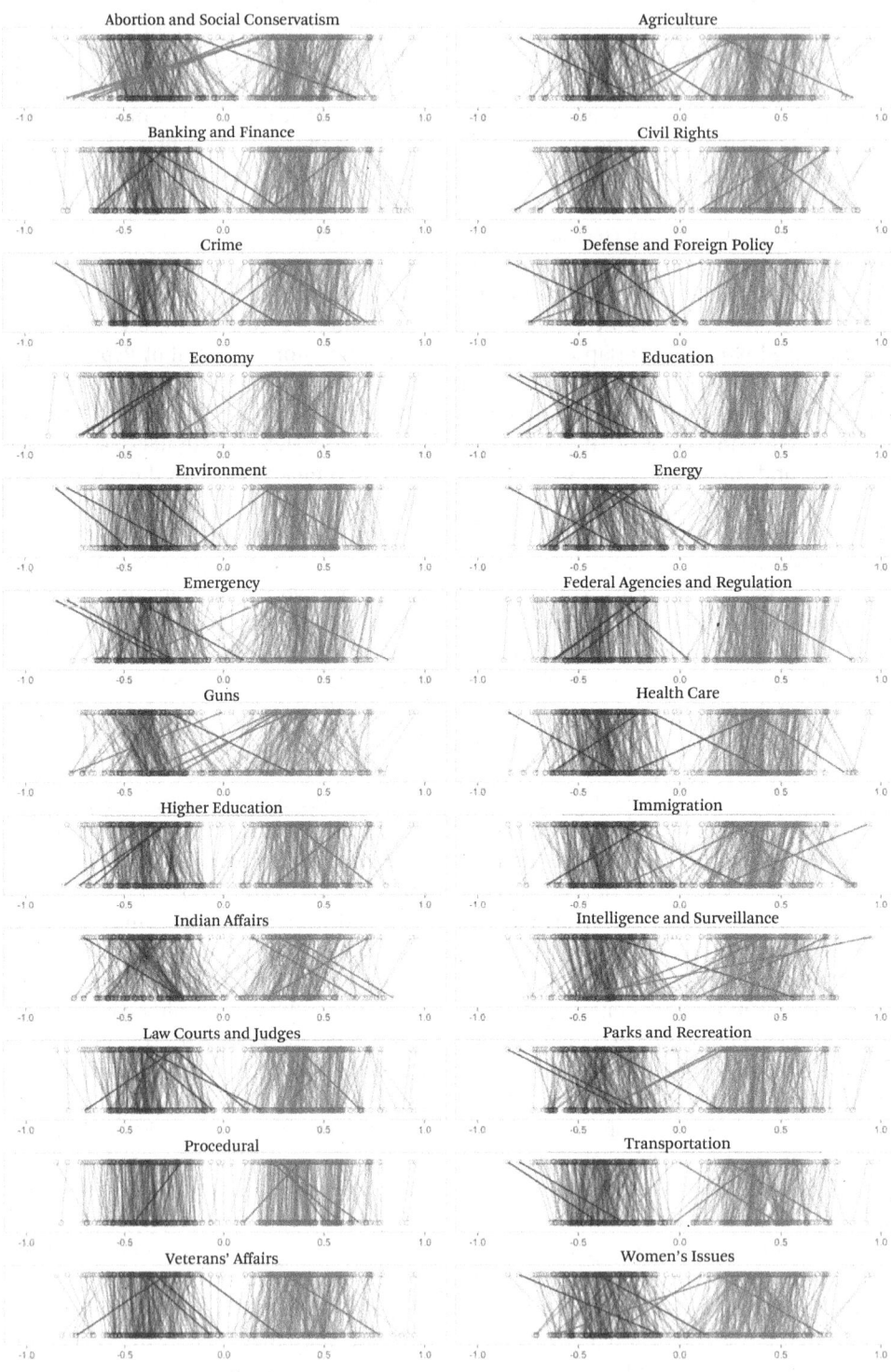

Source: Author's calculations.

Figure 5. Legislator Ideal Points from Classical OC and Issue-Specific OC (113th Congress)

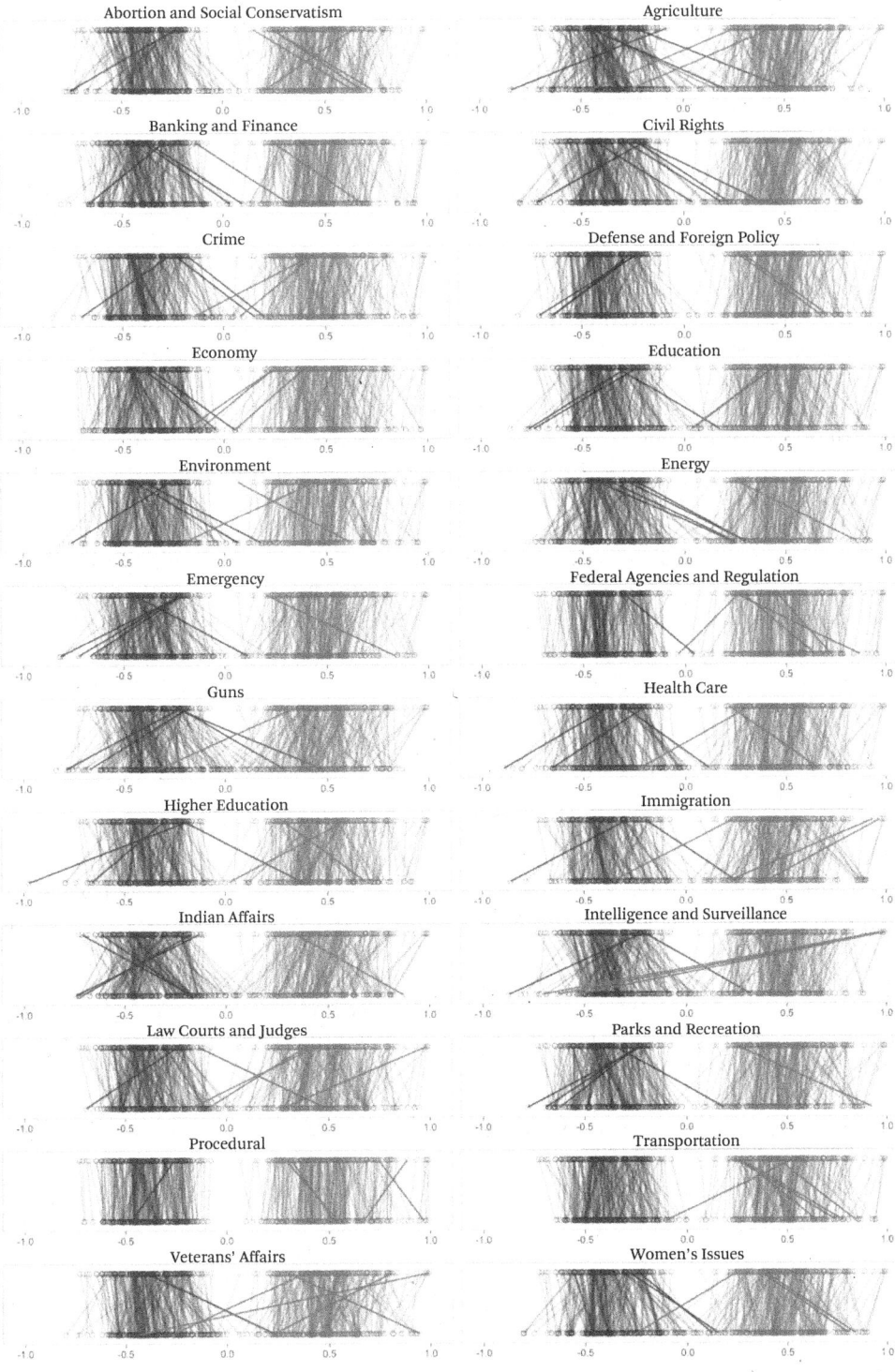

Source: Author's calculations.

regression (SVR) (Drucker et al. 1997; Smola and Schölkopf 2004).[6]

The SVR approach has several advantages. What this approach lacks in elegance is made up for by its extensibility and generalizability. In theory, there is no reason why other types of data could not be included alongside the contribution data as additional features. The model presented here combines contribution records with word frequencies from the document-term matrix for use as the predictor matrix. Although contribution data perform much better than text-as-data when modeled separately, including both data sources boosts cross-validated R-squared by one to two percentage points for most issue dimensions over the contribution matrix alone.

A downside to this approach is that it takes the roll call estimates as known quantities despite the presence of measurement error. Assessing model fit thus becomes somewhat problematic, as the extent to which cross-validation error actually reflects attenuation bias is unclear. Although not ideal, I proceed by treating the roll call estimates as though they are measured without error.[7]

The SVR model is fit using a linear kernel and recursive feature selection. To help the model handle the sparsity in the contribution matrix, I construct an *n*-by-*k* matrix that summarizes the percentage of funds a candidate raised from donors within different ideological deciles. This is done by calculating contributor coordinates from the weighted average of contributions made to the set of candidates with roll call estimates for the target issue scale and then binning the coordinates into deciles. The candidate decile shares are then calculated as the proportion of total funds raised from contributors located within each decile. When calculating the contributor coordinates, contributions made to candidates in the test set are excluded so as not to contaminate the cross-validation results. This simple trick helps to augment feature selection. As is typical with support vector machines, the modeling parameters require careful calibration. The ε and cost parameters are tuned separately for each issue dimension.

Table 3 reports fit statistics for fifteen issue dimensions for members of the 113th Congress. The cross-validated correlation coefficients are above 0.95 for every issue. The within-party correlations are generally above 0.60, indicating that the model can explain variation in the scores of co-partisans.

The SVR model demonstrates the viability of training a machine learning model to learn about candidate issue positions from contribution records and text. The SVR as presented performs quite well for its intended purpose but leaves room for improvement. In most other contexts, the cross-validation results would be a resounding success. In this context, however, the historically high level of issue constraint causes the model to suffer from a "curse of unidimensionality." Candidate positions across issues are so strongly correlated that it becomes a challenge to train a model that is nuanced enough to pick up on variation revealed by the issue-specific OC model, which is often driven by a small fraction of legislators who deviate from their positions on one or two given issue dimensions. Moving forward, ensemble methods that build on the SVR model—k-nearest neighbors methods in particular—show promise for improving predictive performance. It also remains to be seen whether similarly high levels of issue constraint are present in the state legislatures.

A DATA-DRIVEN VOTER GUIDE

In this section, I provide an overview of the design and development of Crowdpac's data-driven voter guide. The initial motivation was to build a tool capable of providing users with objective information on the policy preferences and expressed priorities of a comprehen-

---

6. For a complete treatment of the application of supervised machine learning methods to infer roll call ideology from campaign contributions, see Bonica (2016).

7. An alternative approach worth exploring would be to train a binary classifier on individual vote choices on bills and then scale the predicted vote choices for candidates using the roll call parameters recovered from OC. Although this approach would sidestep issues with measurement error, it would probably present additional challenges.

Table 3. Fit Measures from Cross-Validation on Fifteen Issue Dimensions, 113th Congress

	All		Democrats		Republicans	
	Pearson R	RMSE	Pearson R	RMSE	Pearson R	RMSE
Latent	0.979	0.074	0.819	0.06	0.775	0.085
Defense and foreign policy	0.973	0.085	0.732	0.073	0.740	0.094
Banking and finance	0.973	0.081	0.700	0.076	0.751	0.085
Energy	0.971	0.084	0.711	0.074	0.722	0.092
Health care	0.970	0.091	0.760	0.078	0.741	0.100
Economy	0.968	0.089	0.687	0.081	0.721	0.095
Environment	0.966	0.094	0.680	0.089	0.732	0.095
Women's issues	0.964	0.094	0.619	0.083	0.687	0.101
Education	0.963	0.099	0.679	0.087	0.678	0.108
Abortion and social conservatism	0.961	0.102	0.637	0.096	0.691	0.107
Higher education	0.958	0.104	0.698	0.090	0.697	0.115
Immigration	0.957	0.110	0.643	0.103	0.699	0.115
Fair elections	0.956	0.117	0.626	0.099	0.659	0.139
Intelligence and surveillance	0.952	0.108	0.705	0.088	0.543	0.126
Labor	0.952	0.122	0.603	0.123	0.663	0.123
Guns	0.951	0.116	0.680	0.089	0.560	0.137

Source: Author's calculations.

sive set of candidates. While Crowdpac's voter guide provides an illustrative example of such a tool, the data and techniques employed here are quite flexible and could be extended to produce different types of voter guides.

Figure 6 displays a screenshot that captures three of the eleven primary races appearing on the sample ballot from the Crowdpac voter guide for the 2014 California primary elections. Each candidate in the contest is assigned an overall ideological score ranging from 10L for candidates on the far left to 10C for candidates on the far right. The scores are rescaled to enhance interpretability for users. The rescaling function is identified using the historical averages for the parties in Congress over the past two decades. First, the historical party means are calculated by aggregating over the ideal points of the members from each party serving in each Congress from 1992 to 2012. The scores are then rescaled such that the midpoint between the party means is set to 0 and the historical party means are positioned at 5L and 5C. The scores are windsorized at 10L and 10C. The user interface was designed to scope with respect to the level of detail displayed about a candidate.

The unidimensional scores for candidates are top-level summaries that serve as jumping-off points for exploring more detailed data on them. More inquiring users are given the option to further explore the data by clicking through to the "data details" pages provided for each candidate. Figure 7 displays a screenshot for the data details page for Cory Booker (D-NJ) as an example. The module on the top displays the candidate's ideal point with respect to his opponents in the upcoming election. While the voter guide makes extensive use of scores along a liberal-to-conservative dimension, issue-specific ideal points are also available for a large percentage of candidates who meet the minimum data requirement of raising funds from at least 100 distinct donors who have also donated to one or more other candidates. The bottom modules summarize the candidate's fund-raising activity by showing the distribution of ideal points of donors to his campaign along with other general fund-raising statistics. For candidates who have made personal donations to other candidates and committees, there is a toggle option that shows the ideological distribution of the recipients weighted by amount. Other modules not shown include (1) a visualization of the candidate's fund-raising network accompa-

Figure 6. Screenshot of Sample Ballot from Crowdpac Voter Guide to 2014 California Primary Elections

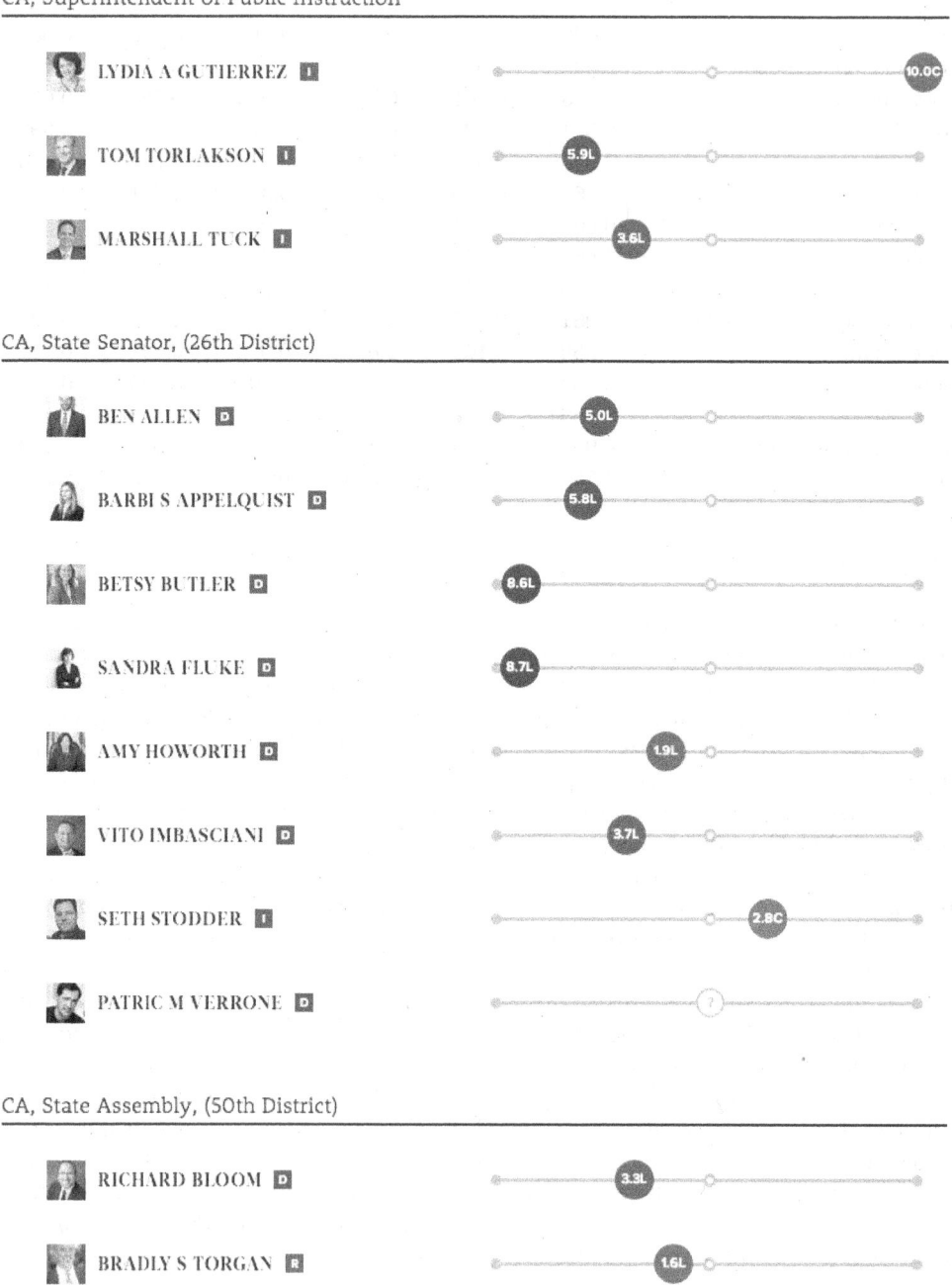

Source: www.crowdpac.com (accessed September 29, 2014).

Figure 7. Screenshot of Data Details Page for Crowdpac's Voter Guide to the Candidate Cory Booker (D-NJ)

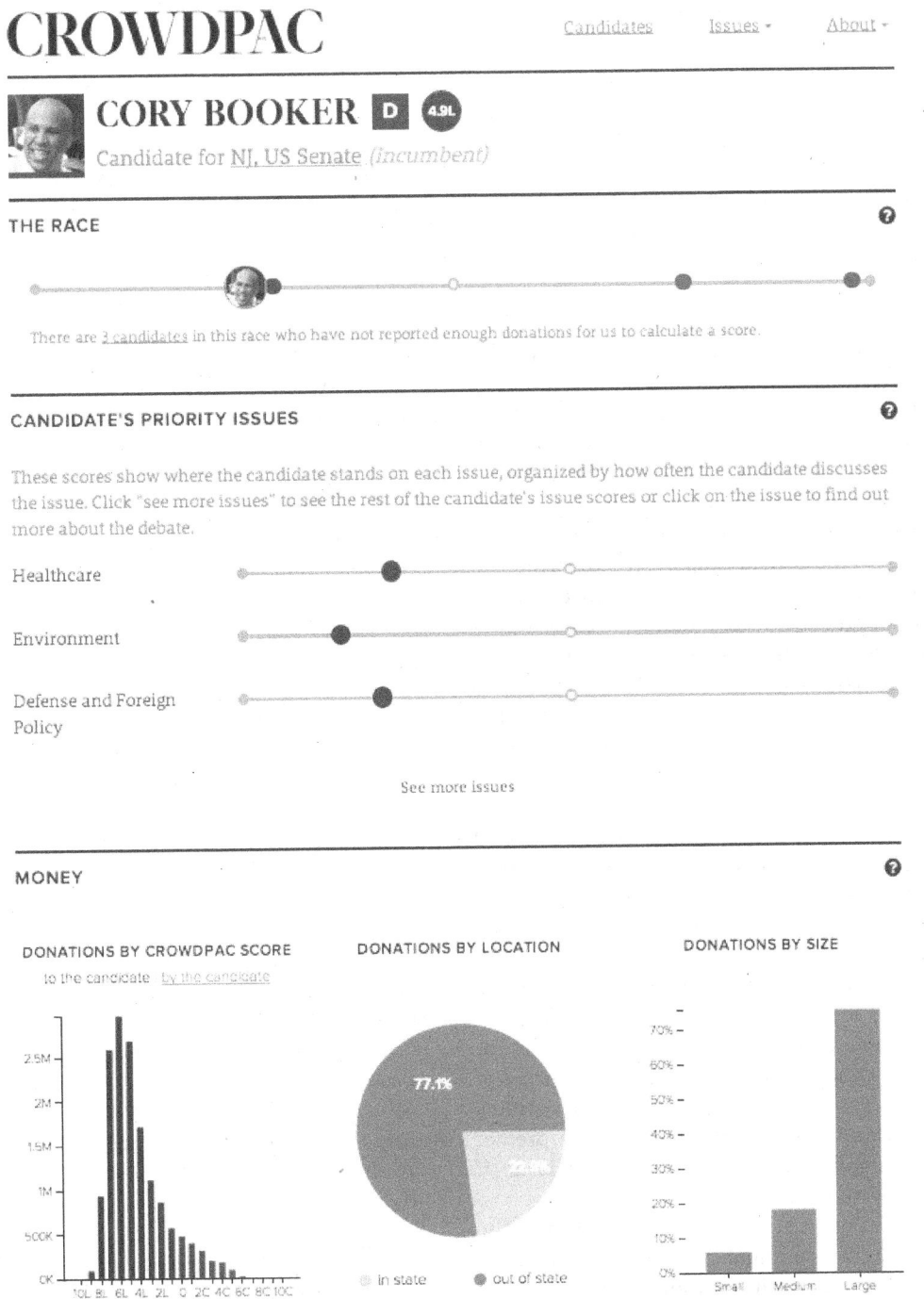

Source: www.crowdpac.com (accessed September 29, 2014).

nied by a listing of the candidate's nearest neighbors (that is, the donors who gave to the candidate and also gave to candidates X, Y, Z); (2) a summary of the candidate's text showing his expressed priorities and a word cloud of top terms; (3) a video of the candidate from YouTube or another video sharing service; (4) biographical information, including past political experience and offices held; and (5) for sitting members of Congress, a summary of recent voting behavior and interest group ratings.

CONCLUSIONS

This paper proposes a scalable strategy for collecting and modeling data on U.S. political elites as a means of measuring the positions and priorities for a comprehensive set of candidates. The project hinges on the ability to collect, process, and organize large amounts of data on candidates and other political elites. Many of the needed support structures for data provision have been institutionalized by disclosure regimes. The initial fixed costs associated with building the tools for automating the process of collecting and processing new data as they become available are considerable, but once paid, the database should yield continued benefits with much reduced maintenance costs.

Although more work remains, the model is able to reliably position candidates along a liberal-to-conservative dimension and capture meaningful variation in legislator ideal points across issue dimensions. By training on the set of ideal points recovered from the issue-specific OC model, a support vector regression model is used to infer scores for other candidates based on shared sources of data. This modeling strategy demonstrates the viability of training a model to predict how candidates would vote on an issue if they were in office.

The potential benefits are twofold. First, the model offers a valuable new data resource for social scientists. In addition to compiling and standardizing data on political candidates, legislative behavior, political text, campaign contributions, and election outcomes in an accessible format, considerable effort has gone into automating data collection and merging and disambiguating data drawn from different sources. The result is a unified data resource on American political elites unprecedented in its size, scope, and variety. Moreover, the data architecture is designed to accommodate the addition of new data sources centered on candidates and political organizations—for example, Twitter follower networks (Barberá 2015) or interest group ratings and endorsements—which would then be automatically linked to each of the other included data sources.

Second, the model provides a means of democratizing political disclosure data by making such data more accessible to citizens. The website design has been built around the founding principle that, as with almost any activity, most citizens want to minimize the time and effort they spend on politics while maximizing their effectiveness. If successful, the model could promote political engagement by lowering information costs, reducing uncertainty, and enhancing efficacy.

REFERENCES

Aldrich, John H., and Richard D. McKelvey. 1977. "A Method of Scaling with Applications to the 1968 and 1972 Presidential Elections." *American Political Science Review* 71(1): 111–30.

Alvarez, R. Michael, Ines Levin, Peter Mair, and Alexander H. Trechsel. 2014. "Party Preferences in the Digital Age: The Impact of Voting Advice Applications." *Party Politics* 20(2): 227–36.

Ansolabehere, Stephen, Jr., James M. Snyder, and Charles Stewart III. 2001. "Candidate Positioning in U.S. House Elections." *American Journal of Political Science* 45(1): 136–59.

Bailey, Michael A. 2007. "Comparable Preference Estimates Across Time and Institutions for the Court, Congress, and Presidency." *American Journal of Political Science* 51(3): 433–48.

Barberá, Pablo. 2015. "Birds of the Same Feather Tweet Together: Bayesian Ideal Point Estimation Using Twitter Data." *Political Analysis* 23(1): 76–91.

Blackwell, Matthew, James Honaker, and Gary King. 2010. "Multiple Overimputation: A Unified Approach to Measurement Error and Missing Data." Working paper. July 19. Available at: http://polmeth.wustl.edu/files/polmeth/measure.pdf (accessed May 31, 2016).

Bonica, Adam. 2014. "Mapping the Ideological Marketplace." *American Journal of Political Science* 58(2): 367–87.

———. 2016. "Inferring Roll Call Scores from Campaign Contributions Using Supervised Machine Learning." Working paper. Stanford, Calif.: Stanford University (Mach 12). Available at: SSRN: http://ssrn.com/abstract=2732913 (accessed May 31, 2016).

Burden, Barry C. 2004. "Candidate Positioning in U.S. Congressional Elections." *British Journal of Political Science* 34(2): 211–27.

Clark, Tom S., and Benjamin Lauderdale. 2012. "The Supreme Court's Many Median Justices." *American Political Science Review* 106(4): 847–66.

Drucker, Harris, Chris J. C. Burges, Linda Kaufman, Alex Smola, and Vladimir Vapnik. 1997. "Support Vector Regression Machines." *Advances in Neural Information Processing Systems* 9: 155–61.

Epstein, Lee, Andrew D. Martin, Jeffrey A. Segal, and Chad Westerland. 2007. "The Judicial Common Space." *Journal of Law, Economics, and Organization* 23(2): 303–25.

Gerrish, Sean, and David M. Blei. 2012. "How They Vote: Issue-Adjusted Models of Legislative Behavior." *Advances in Neural Information Processing Systems* 25: 2753–61.

Grimmer, Justin. 2010. "A Bayesian Hierarchical Topic Model for Political Texts: Measuring Expressed Agendas in Senate Press Releases." *Political Analysis* 18(1): 1–35.

Grimmer, Justin, and Brandon M. Stewart. 2013. "Text as Data: The Promise and Pitfalls of Automatic Content Analysis Methods for Political Texts." *Political Analysis*, 1–31. doi: 10.1093/pan/mps028.

Hare, Christopher, David A. Armstrong, Ryan Bakker, Royce Carroll, and Keith T. Poole. 2014. "Using Bayesian Aldrich-McKelvey Scaling to Study Citizens' Ideological Preferences and Perceptions." *American Journal of Political Science* 59(3): 759–74.

Issenberg, Sasha. 2012. *The Victory Lab: The Secret Science of Winning Campaigns*. New York: Random House.

Ladner, Andreas, Gabriela Felder, and Jan Fivaz. 2010. "More Than Toys? A First Assessment of Voting Advice Applications in Switzerland." In *Voting Advice Applications in Europe: The State of the Art*, edited by Lorella Cedroni and Diego Garcia. Naples: ScriptaWeb.

Lauderdale, Benjamin, and Tom S. Clark. 2014. "Scaling Politically Meaningful Dimensions Using Texts and Votes." *American Journal of Political Science* 58(3): 754–71.

Laver, Michael, Kenneth Benoit, and John Garry. 2003. "Extracting Policy Positions from Political Texts Using Words as Data." *American Political Science Review* 92(2): 311–32.

Louwerse, Tom, and Martin Rosema. 2013. "The Design Effects of Voting Advice Applications: Comparing Methods of Calculating Matches." *Acta Politica* (October 18). doi:10.1057/ap.2013.30.

Martin, Andrew D., and Kevin M. Quinn. 2002. "Dynamic Ideal Point Estimation via Markov Chain Monte Carlo for the U.S. Supreme Court, 1953–1999." *Political Analysis* 10(2): 134–53.

McCarty, Nolan M., and Keith T. Poole. 1998. "An Empirical Spatial Model of Congressional Campaigns." *Political Analysis* 7(1): 1–30.

Monroe, Burt L., Michael P. Colaresi, and Kevin M. Quinn. 2008. "Fightin' Words: Lexical Feature Selection and Evaluation for Identifying the Content of Political Conflict." *Political Analysis* 16(4): 372–403.

Monroe, Burt L., and Ko Maeda. 2004. "Talk's Cheap: Text Based Estimation of Rhetorical Ideal-Points." Paper presented to the Twenty-First Annual Summer Meeting of the Society for Political Methodology. Stanford University (July 29–31).

Peress, Michael. 2013. "Estimating Proposal and Status Quo Locations Using Voting and Cosponsorship Data." *Journal of Politics* 75(3): 613–31.

Poole, Keith T. 2000. "Nonparametric Unfolding of Binary Choice Data." *Political Analysis* 8(3): 211–37.

Poole, Keith, Jeffrey Lewis, James Lo, and Royce Carroll. 2011. "Scaling Roll Call Votes with WNOMINATE in R." *Journal of Statistical Software* 42(14): 1–21.

Poole, Keith T., and Howard Rosenthal. 1985. "A Spatial Model for Legislative Roll Call Analysis." *American Journal of Political Science* 29(2): 357–84.

———. 1997. *Congress: A Political-Economic History of Roll Call Voting*. New York: Oxford University Press.

Ramage, Daniel, Christopher D. Manning, and Susan Dumais. 2011. "Partially Labeled Topic Models for Interpretable Text Mining." In Association for Computing Machinery (ACM), *Proceedings of the 17th ACM SIGKDD International*

Conference on Knowledge Discovery and Data Mining (San Diego, Calif., August 21–24), 457–65.

Ramage, Daniel, Evan Rosen, Jason Chuang, Christopher D. Manning, and Daniel A. McFarland. 2009. "Topic Modeling for the Social Sciences." Presented at Neural Information Processing Systems (NIPS) 2009 Workshop on Applications for Topic Models: Text and Beyond. Whistler, Canada (December).

Roberts, Margaret E., Brandon M. Stewart, Dustin Tingley, Christopher Lucas, Jetson Leder-Luis, Shana Kushner Gadarian, Bethany Albertson, and David G. Rand. 2014. "Structural Topic Models for Open-Ended Survey Responses." *American Journal of Political Science* 58(4): 1064–82.

Rosema, Martin, Joel Anderson, and Stefaan Walgrave. 2014. "The Design, Purpose, and Effects of Voting Advice Applications." *Electoral Studies* (36): 240–43.

Shor, Boris, and Nolan M. McCarty. 2011. "The Ideological Mapping of American Legislatures." *American Political Science Review* 105(3): 530–51.

Slapin, Jonathan B., and Sven-Oliver Proksch. 2008. "A Scaling Model for Estimating Time-Series Party Positions from Texts." *American Journal of Political Science* 52(3): 705–22.

Smola, Alex J., and Bernhard Schölkopf. 2004. "A Tutorial on Support Vector Regression." *Statistics and Computing* 14(3): 199–222.

Willis, Derek. 2014. "New Voter Guide Follows the Money." *New York Times*, September 1.

Income, Ideology, and Representation

CHRIS TAUSANOVITCH

Do legislators represent the rich better than they represent the poor? Recent work provides mixed support for this proposition. I test the hypothesis of differential representation using a data set on the political preferences of 318,537 individuals. Evidence of differential representation in the House of Representatives is weak. Support for differential representation is stronger in the Senate. In recent years, representation has occurred primarily through the selection of a legislator from the appropriate party. Although the preferences of higher-income constituents account for more of the variation in legislator voting behavior, higher-income constituents also account for much more of the variation in district preferences. In light of the low level of overall responsiveness, differential responsiveness appears small.

Keywords: representation, ideology, Congress

Few issues in the study of representation have garnered more attention in recent years than the link between economic inequality and political inequality. The majority view in this literature argues that government responds to the preferences of large segments of the population that are higher income much more than it responds to large segments of the population that are lower income (Bartels 2009; Bonica et al. 2013; Butler 2014; Gilens 2012; Gilens and Page 2014). This finding implies that even though citizens are equal in their ability to vote, they are unequal in their ability to incentivize politicians to take particular policy positions. That this difference remains even after accounting for different rates of voting (Bartels 2009) begs the question of why legislators would ignore a substantial portion of the people to whom they owe their jobs and continued reelection.

The approach pioneered by Larry Bartels (2009) is useful for answering this question. Bartels examines the dyadic relationship between legislators and different classes of constituents within their districts. He supposes that legislators vote according to the wishes of their mean voter, as per various "mean voter theorems" (see, for example, Caplin and Nalebuff 1991; Schofield 2007). If this is the case, then each citizen should receive equal weight in a legislator's voting decision, just as each quantity is weighted equally in the calculation of an arithmetic mean. Groups should be weighted in correspondence with their individual size. Given a set of non-overlapping groups, this assumption leads to a clear speci-

---

Chris Tausanovitch is assistant professor in the Department of Political Science at the University of California–Los Angeles.

This work builds on work in my dissertation that benefited greatly from comments and feedback from David Brady, Morris Fiorina, Simon Jackman, Jeffrey B. Lewis, and Howard Rosenthal. It also builds on work with Jeffrey Lewis creating the software necessary to estimate the model of preferences. All mistakes remain my own. Direct correspondence to: Chris Tausanovitch at ctausanovitch@ucla.edu, 3383 Bunche Hall, University of California–Los Angeles, CA 90095.

fication for determining whether legislators do weight groups equally: assume that legislator positions are a function of the positions of the mean of each group multiplied by each group's relative size, but allow the actual weights to vary.

However, representing the mean voter is not the only way that legislators may make their decision. The mean voter theorem replaces the older and more prominent theory of representation of the median voter (Black 1948; Downs 1957). If legislators represent the median voter, they may have equal regard for all of their constituents, but nonetheless some will seem to receive more "weight" than others—in particular, those constituents who vary more or are otherwise more likely to determine the location of the median. Yet another way in which legislators may represent their districts is via the mediating effects of party (Campbell et al. 1966). Voters may simply choose a candidate of the party they prefer, and conditional on choosing the right party, legislators may be bound only by the standards of loyal behavior within that party. If legislators have this degree of latitude, then whichever group is most likely to determine the balance of party support within a district will appear to have the greatest weight, despite an equal regard for all voters by the legislator.

In this paper, I test the hypothesis of differential representation in the U.S. House of Representatives and the U.S. Senate. For some House sessions I am able to replicate the existing result of differential representation using a large data set of political preferences. However, I also show, following two recent papers using other data sources (Bhatti and Erikson 2011; Brunner, Ross, and Washington 2013), that this result is not robust and depends on whether the slope or the fit of the model is thought to be a better indicator of responsiveness. More importantly, I show that these models do not necessarily imply large substantive differences in legislator positions resulting from differential representation. In univariate models, all groups are substantially predictive of the position that legislators will take.

In the Senate, I consistently find a stronger relationship between the preferences of richer constituents and the positions of legislators. The coefficients are somewhat uncertain, however, owing to very high multicollinearity. This finding is consistent with prior work that finds greater representation of the rich in the Senate (Bartels 2009). Nonetheless, the results highlight one of the concerns of Yosef Bhatti and Robert Erikson (2011), namely, that the preferences of various income groups are difficult to separate statistically.

In direct contrast to the mean voter theorem—the theoretical assumption underlying Bartels's (2009) empirical specification—legislator positions were relatively homogenous within parties and heterogenous across parties from 2000 to 2012, and that continues to be true as of this writing. Partisan theories of representation are a reasonable alternative that do a better job of matching this empirical reality. Perhaps groups are unequal in the extent to which they determine the party of their representative. This result leads to a different empirical specification of party, not legislator position, as the dependent variable (Brunner, Ross, and Washington 2013). In the latter part of the paper, I show that this specification leads to a similar conclusion. The positions of both low-income and high-income constituents explain the party of their representative reasonably well in the House, with more evidence of differential representation in the Senate. The slope of this relationship is steeper for higher-income constituents. Discriminating between different explanations for legislator behavior is a difficult task that is beyond the scope of this paper. Nonetheless, the fact that these two very different approaches give similar results is a useful starting point.

These results should be understood in the context of broader political realities. The correspondence between the political preferences of constituencies writ large and the preferences of their representatives is remarkably weak, particularly when party is accounted for (Clinton 2006; Tausanovitch and Warshaw 2013). During a period when Congress has polarized dramatically, the distribution of the public's preferences has remained centrist and stable, highlighting this disconnect (Fiorina and Abrams 2012; Hill and Tausanovitch 2015). In other words, responsiveness at an aggregate level appears to be poor. This is not surprising in light of recent evidence that casts doubt on the notion that a significant number of voters choose candidates on the basis of policy (Tausanovitch and Warshaw 2014). Furthermore, few voters are aware of the policy stances of their particular representatives above and beyond differences between the two parties (Tausanovitch and Warshaw 2014).

In light of these findings, one might wonder whether disaggregating constituents into high- and low-income groups could provide an explanation. After all, if legislators respond only to high-income constituents, then "averaging in" lower-income constituents will create the appearance of weaker representation. The results reported here show that this does not appear to be the case. Separating groups by income and introducing income itself as an additional variable does not appear to substantially improve our ability to predict the positions that legislators will take.

In the section that follows, I explain the methodology I use to estimate policy positions. Then I go on to describe the data underlying the analysis. The next two sections present the results on mean voter representation and on partisan representation, followed by the conclusion.

MEASURING PREFERENCES

One of the core difficulties in measuring policy preferences is that statements of preferences on individual issues may not accurately reflect underlying attitudes. Respondents may make top-of-the-head judgments based on immediately available considerations (Zaller 1992), or their choice may be affected by purely idiosyncratic or irrelevant factors (see, for example, Achen and Bartels 2012). One possible solution to this problem is to aggregate preferences in some way. Multiple (putatively) independent indicators of political preferences are less affected by random noise than a single response. Research has shown that using multiple indicators increases the predictive power of voters' attitudes on outcomes such as vote choice (Ansolabehere, Rodden, and Snyder 2008).

The most commonly used methods for measuring underlying positions from revealed preference data are item response models, which conceptualize preferences as a continuous latent variable in an underlying preference space. Individual choices depend on the choosers' latent preferences and the features of that particular choice. One of the simplest cases is a one-dimensional quadratic utility binary response model (Clinton, Jackman, and Rivers 2004). Let x_i denote person i's latent ideology, and y_{ij} denote person i's response to question j, where $y_{ij} = 1$ indicates a "yes" response and $y_{ij} = 0$ indicates a "no" response to question j. Then the probability that person i will respond "yes" to question j is

$$Pr(y_{ij} = 1) = \Phi(\beta_j x_i - \alpha_j)$$

where Φ is the standard normal cumulative distribution function, and α_j and β_j are the item parameters for question j. β_j captures the direction of the item (is "yes" a liberal or conservative response?) as well as how strong the relationship is between responses to the item and underlying preferences. α_j captures the underlying liberalism or conservatism of the item (how liberal does one typically have to be to respond "yes" or "no"?). The model is identified by restricting the x_i's to have mean 0 and standard deviation 1, and the direction is fixed so that negative values are liberal.

This simple model allows us to estimate preferences and take account of the fact that some questions are more informative than others in different parts of the preference space. I estimate this model using a Bayesian approach, with dispersed normal priors for each of the estimated parameters. Unfortunately, it is quite computationally expensive to run in standard implementation. Using software developed with Jeffrey B. Lewis of UCLA, I parallelize a Markov chain Monte Carlo estimate of this model using data augmentation. In each iteration of the Markov chain, posterior draws from the distribution of the item parameters and person parameters can be made independently. We conduct these draws simultaneously on graphical processing units (GPUs), allowing us to achieve speeds thirty-two times faster than standard implementations of this model. Using this software, I am able to estimate latent preferences for a data set of 318,537 survey respondents, containing 5,084,676 nonmissing responses to 264 items.

There are numerous advantages to using a continuous measure of political preferences based on responses to policy questions, but the most important one is that a continuous measure of preferences simply gives us more information about the location of individuals in the policy space. This may be the reason that Bhatti and Erikson (2011) are able to find differential representation in the Senate using the 9,253 respondents to the American National Election Study (ANES) with a seven-point measure of ideological self-placement, but unable to find differential representation using the 155,000 respondents to the National Annenberg Election Survey (NAES) with a five-point measure. The less granular measure does not distinguish as well. An added benefit of the measurement strategy used here is that using multiple items may mitigate measurement error.

DATA

Analyzing representation requires data on the policy preferences of constituents and the legislators who represent them. Data on the former come from six large-sample political surveys: the 2000 and 2004 National Annenberg Election Surveys, and the 2006, 2008, 2010, and 2012 Cooperative Congressional Election Studies (CCES). Combined, these studies provide responses from 318,537 individuals over this period of twelve years, for an average of 732 respondents in each of the 435 congressional districts.

The household income of respondents is self-reported on each survey in a series of categories. However, the categories differ across the NAES and CCES, and the sixteen CCES categories were changed in 2012. When the categories were consolidated into four groups, they perfectly coincided, with the exception of the 2012 CCES. These four groups comprise those making less than $25,000, those making $25,000 to $49,999, those making $50,000 to $99,999, and those making more than $100,000. I call these groups "low-income," "medium-low-income," "medium-high-income," and "high-income," respectively. With 78 percent of respondents choosing to answer the income question, the sample was reduced to 282,701. Twenty percent of respondents are classified as low-income, 27.6 percent as medium-low-income, 33.6 percent as medium-high-income, and 16.5 percent as high-income. For the 2012 CCES, the boundary defining low and medium-low income is $30,000 instead of $25,000. For the analysis in the main text, I include the 2012 CCES data, but in the appendix I replicate all of the results excuding these data; the results are largely unchanged.

There are 264 unique policy questions in this data set. However, responses to these questions are sparse owing to the fact that different surveys ask different policy questions. Following Tausanovitch and Warshaw (2013), I identify the positions of respondents to different surveys relative to one another by constraining common questions to have the same item parameters.[1] In addition, I use smaller sample surveys attached to the large 2010 and 2011 CCES surveys to provide more linking questions. The purpose of these surveys was to ask 177 of the questions that had been asked in prior surveys in order to estimate the item parameters in a common space. Later surveys are linked using these questions and common questions on the CCES. This method for linking large sample surveys and the data for doing so come from Tausanovitch and Warshaw (2013).

Data for the positions of legislators come from Keith Poole and Howard Rosenthal's DW-NOMINATE scores (Poole and Rosenthal 1997).[2] Although the functional form of DW-NOMINATE is different from the Bayesian quadratic item response model outlined here, in practice it results in very similar estimates, and so for convenience I use it here. Rather than respond to survey questions, members of Congress cast roll call votes on policy issues. DW-NOMINATE scores are calculated using members' roll call votes as their statements of

---

1. This assumption may not be correct if, for instance, the interpretation of the items changes over time. Although testing this assumption is beyond the scope of this paper, see Lewis and Tausanovitch (2013).

2. Data provided at the Voteview website (www.voteview.com, accessed August 2014).

Table 1. Pearson Correlations Between Mean Preferences of Income Groups Within Congressional Districts

	μ_H	μ_{MH}	μ_{ML}	μ_L
μ_{MH}	0.87			
μ_{ML}	0.84	0.90		
μ_L	0.75	0.81	0.80	
μ	0.92	0.97	0.95	0.86

Source: Author's calculations based on the 2000 and 2004 National Annenberg Election Surveys (Annenberg Public Policy Center 2000 and 2004) and the 2006, 2008, 2010, and 2012 Cooperative Congressional Election Studies (Ansolabehere 2010a, 2010b, 2012; Ansolabehere and Schaffner 2013) as well as the author's original modules on the 2010 and 2011 Cooperative Congressional Election Studies.
Note: N = 435. In all cases, $p < .001$.

preference. Since these votes are actually yes-or-no choices, they are amenable to a binary model.

In the main analysis, districts are matched to their respective members of the House of Representatives and the Senate for the 111th Congress (2009–2011). The choice of Congress is somewhat arbitrary, because survey data are drawn from a period covering six congressional elections. Using each possible legislator-district pair over this period would be, in a sense, double-counting observations. In the appendix, I rerun the analysis using every Congress from the 106th through the 112th—all of the sessions that used the year 2000 census districts. I comment on important discrepancies between these results and the results reported in the main text where appropriate.

Prior work on this topic focuses on the Senate owing to sample size constraints (Bartels 2009; Bhatti and Erikson 2011). I focus on the House, while replicating my analysis for the Senate. The Senate analysis is more consistent with previous findings. At the same time, greater multicollinearity and fewer legislator observations make the Senate results more uncertain.

The CCES provides district identifiers for each respondent. For the NAES, I match respondents probabilistically to their districts using their zip codes. Most zip codes are fully contained within districts, but where there is partial overlap with multiple districts, the extent of the overlap is used to calculate the probability that a given respondent resides in a given district. Districts are from the year 2000 redistricting.

RESULTS: INCOME AND REPRESENTATION

Is it in fact the case that higher-income voters are better represented than lower-income voters? Although more attention has been given to those arguing in the affirmative, there are some nicely executed counterexamples. Using much larger sample sizes than the original Bartels (2009) study, both Bhatti and Erikson (2011) and Brunner, Ross, and Washington (2013) find mixed evidence of differential representation. Both studies have disadvantages. Bhatti and Erikson (2011) use respondents' self-placement using abstract ideological labels ("very liberal," "liberal," "moderate," "conservative," and "very conservative") as the measure of respondent positions. Brunner, Ross, and Washington (2013) use ballot propositions to measure voter ideology, but there are a limited number of such propositions in each election; in addition, they measure income at the neighborhood level, in California only. Nonetheless, their data come from the universe of voters, and as a result their sample size is enviable. In contrast to these papers, I use a large national sample of individuals responding to large numbers of policy questions, with income measured at the individual level.

Why have existing studies come to different conclusions regarding representation? One explanation is that the variables that we seek to distinguish are highly collinear and measured

Table 2. Pearson Correlations Between Mean Preferences of Income Groups Within States

	μ_H	μ_{MH}	μ_{ML}	μ_L
μ_H				
μ_{MH}	0.92			
μ_{ML}	0.87	0.95		
μ_L	0.81	0.88	0.91	
μ	0.93	0.98	0.97	0.93

Source: Author's calculations based on the 2000 and 2004 National Annenberg Election Surveys (Annenberg Public Policy Center 2000 and 2004) and the 2006, 2008, 2010, and 2012 Cooperative Congressional Election Studies (Ansolabehere 2010a, 2010b, 2012; Ansolabehere and Schaffner 2013) as well as the author's original modules on the 2010 and 2011 Cooperative Congressional Election Studies.
Note: N = 50. In all cases, $p < .001$.

with error. Table 1 shows the pairwise correlations between five variables in U.S. House districts. μ_H is the mean preferences of high-income constituents (annual income more than $100,000), μ_{MH} is the mean preferences of medium-high-income constituents ($50,000 to $99,999), μ_{ML} is the mean preferences of medium-low-income constituents ($25,000 to $49,999), and μ_L is the mean preferences of low-income constituents (less than $25,000). The mean preferences of all constituents is μ. The lowest correlations are between the preferences of low-income constituents and other groups, but all of these correlations are very high. Unlike past studies, these measures reduce error through the use of a measurement model. Nonetheless, all of the quantities are measured with error that is due in part to measurement and in part to sampling. High correlations between each quantity raise the possibility of autocorrelated error, which can cause instability in regression coefficients. Table 2 shows that the corresponding multicollinearity in the Senate is even more problematic.

I begin by replicating the methodology used by Bartels (2009), using the data for the Senate. In each district I calculate the percentage of the sample that falls into each group. I call this p_g, where g indexes the group L, ML, MH, and H, respectively. I then decompose the mean preferences of the district into the means of each group, multiplied by the proportion in that group. By Bartels's logic, if legislators represent mean preferences in their district without regard to income, then the coefficients in a regression of legislator position on the proportion-weighted group means should all be equal. If the coefficient on one group is higher than the others, this is consistent with the hypothesis that legislators change their positions more in response to this group than to the others.

Table 3 shows the results of three regressions for the 111th Senate. The first two are univariate models that simply regress the position of the legislator on the preferences of low-income and high-income people, respectively. The third is the specification from Bartels (2009) that includes each group and weights them by their proportion in the district. The first two models show that both the preferences of the poor and the preferences of the rich are related to legislator positions. However, model 3 is consistent with Bartels's argument. When each income group is included in the model, multiplied by their proportion in the district, only the preferences of the high-income group are significantly related to the positions of the legislator. The preferences of the rich have a signficantly greater effect than the preferences of the poor, and in fact it appears that the poor have no effect at all. These findings hold regardless of which Congress we examine from the 106th to the 112th, as shown in the appendix.

Table 4 shows the same models for the House of Representatives. By Bartels's criteria,

Table 3. Regression of Legislator Position on Income Group Preferences in the U.S. Senate

	Legislator DW-NOMINATE Score		
	(1)	(2)	(3)
μ_L	1.44***		
	(0.22)		
μ_H		0.99***	
		(0.12)	
$\rho_H \times \mu_H$			4.41**
			(1.84)
$\rho_{MH} \times \mu_{MH}$			0.29
			(1.59)
$\rho_{ML} \times \mu_{ML}$			2.06
			(2.05)
$\rho_L \times \mu_L$			-0.57
			(2.49)
Constant	0.24***	-0.17***	-0.12
	(0.05)	(0.04)	(0.10)
Observations	107	107	107
R^2	0.29	0.40	0.43
Adjusted R^2	0.29	0.39	0.41

Source: Author's calculations based on the 2000 and 2004 National Annenberg Election Surveys (Annenberg Public Policy Center 2000 and 2004) and the 2006, 2008, 2010, and 2012 Cooperative Congressional Election Studies (Ansolabehere 2010a, 2010b, 2012; Ansolabehere and Schaffner 2013) as well as the author's original modules on the 2010 and 2011 Cooperative Congressional Election Studies. Legislator positions are Poole and Rosenthal's DW-NOMINATE scores from www.voteview.com.

Note: Unites are legislator-states. The dependent variable is legislator ideological position. μ = mean preferences of each income group by income in each state; L = low-income constituents; ML = medium-low-income constituents; H = high-income constituents; ρ = proportion of the population in each group.

*$p < .1$; **$p < .05$; ***$p < .01$

this model refutes the hypothesis that the rich are better represented than the poor in the House. On the contrary, if anything, low-income people appear to be better represented. Not only is the coefficient in model 1 for low-income preferences greater than the coefficient in model 2 for high-income preferences, but in the combined specification the lowest income group has the greatest coefficient. The effects in model 3 have an oddly nonlinear pattern: the poor garner the greatest coefficient, but the medium-low-income group receives a coefficient that is indistinguishable from 0. This is contrary to any expectation from the literature, and to my own expectation. Once again, the appendix shows that the findings of seemingly greater representation of the poor are consistent across sessions of Congress. (The other coefficients vary substantially.) What could explain these results?

One possibility is that the proportions of rich and poor constituents are variables that capture the urban/rural split that we observe when we divide districts represented by Democrats from those represented by Republicans. The variance of preferences among the poor is much lower than the variance of preferences among the rich, probably because of greater measurement error in the preferences of the poor. However, the proportion of the poor who cross a threshold of "liberalness" may be a good indicator of an urban district, a poor district, or a majority minority district. Rather than gather detailed district-level data, we can account for this sort of possibility by simply controlling for the proportions of the district sample that are in each income group. Table 5 does just this, replicating each column from table 4 but with controls for the proportion high-, low-, and medium-low-income, with medium-high-income as the excluded category. This specification is similar to the one used by Bhatti and Erikson (2011).

The results from table 5 are much more intuitive than the results from table 4, as well as closer to previous findings. Controlling for the income of a district, legislator responsiveness appears to increase with the income of each group. However, these coefficients are not significantly different from one another. Furthermore, the results are not consistent across dif-

Table 4. Regression of Legislator Position on Income Group Preferences in the U.S. House of Representatives

	Legislator DW-NOMINATE Score		
	(1)	(2)	(3)
μ_L	1.206***		
	(0.07)		
μ_H		0.71***	
		(0.04)	
$\rho_H \times \mu_H$			1.46***
			(0.36)
$\rho_{MH} \times \mu_{MH}$			0.93***
			(0.32)
$\rho_{ML} \times \mu_{ML}$			0.32
			(0.40)
$\rho_L \times \mu_L$			2.67***
			(0.52)
Constant	0.27***	−0.09***	0.08***
	(0.02)	(0.02)	(0.03)
Observations	445	445	445
R^2	0.40	0.43	0.53
Adjusted R^2	0.39	0.42	0.52

Source: Author's calculations based on the 2000 and 2004 National Annenberg Election Surveys (Annenberg Public Policy Center 2000 and 2004) and the 2006, 2008, 2010, and 2012 Cooperative Congressional Election Studies (Ansolabehere 2010a, 2010b, 2012; Ansolabehere and Schaffner 2013) as well as the author's original modules on the 2010 and 2011 Cooperative Congressional Election Studies. Legislator positions are Poole and Rosenthal's DW-NOMINATE scores from www.voteview.com.

Note: Unites are legislator-states. The dependent variable is legislator ideological position. μ = mean preferences of each income group by income in each state; L = low-income constituents; ML = medium-low-income constituents; H = high-income constituents; ρ = proportion of the population in each group.

*$p < .1$; **$p < .05$; ***$p < .01$

ferent sessions of Congress. In the appendix, I show that the results from the 106th and 107th Congresses place greater weight on the middle-income groups and the least weight on the high-income group.

Given the ambiguity of the results in tables 4 and 5, it is too soon to conclude that the poor are dramatically underrepresented in the House of Representatives. Research tends more often than not to find that the poor are underrepresented in the Senate, but studying the House has not generalized this conclusion. However, the coefficients in these regressions are not the only way in which we can conceptualize responsiveness or representation.

The approach taken to examining responsiveness so far assumes that the coefficient on group-level preferences is the best measure of whether legislators are "responding" to voter preferences. It is difficult to know how to interpret this coefficient. Legislator positions and voter positions are measured quite differently, and so a larger coefficient could measure overreactions to constituent preferences as easily as it measures better representation. One simple question we might ask is whether the positions of the poor or the rich are more accurate predictors of legislative positions. If legislators are truly focusing on one group more than the other, then our predictions of legislator positions should be closer to the truth when we use the preferences of the better-represented group as a regressor. The evidence on this question from tables 4 and 5 is clear: the variance explained is always higher using the high-income group than the low-income group. This holds for the Senate as well.

To understand what this means exactly, consider figure 1. This figure graphs the univariate regression line of legislator positions on the positions of high-income constituents, overlaid on the scatterplot of the data, for the House. The gray lines in the figure show the regression lines for Republican legislators only (the top cloud) and Democratic legislators only (the bottom cloud). The reason for showing these regression lines should be clear from the plot. The relationship between legislator and constituent positions is hardly linear. The po-

Table 5. Regressions Explaining Legislator Position in the U.S. House of Representatives, Controlling for Income-Only Variables

	Legislator DW-NOMINATE Score		
	(1)	(2)	(3)
μ_L	1.38***		
	(0.08)		
μ_H		0.76***	
		(0.04)	
ρ_H	0.51	0.66	1.40**
	(0.60)	(0.59)	(0.56)
ρ_L	−1.77***	−1.50***	−0.69
	(0.48)	(0.48)	(0.45)
ρ_{ML}	0.82	0.93	0.84
	(0.78)	(0.76)	(0.71)
$\rho_H \times \mu_H$			1.54***
			(0.36)
$\rho_{MH} \times \mu_{MH}$			1.34***
			(0.31)
$\rho_{ML} \times \mu_{ML}$			0.97**
			(0.40)
$\rho_L \times \mu_L$			0.89
			(0.56)
Constant	0.35	−0.15	−0.31
	(0.34)	(0.33)	(0.32)
Observations	445	445	445
R^2	0.46	0.48	0.58
Adjusted R^2	0.46	0.48	0.57

Source: Author's calculations based on the 2000 and 2004 National Annenberg Election Surveys (Annenberg Public Policy Center 2000 and 2004) and the 2006, 2008, 2010, and 2012 Cooperative Congressional Election Studies (Ansolabehere 2010a, 2010b, 2012; Ansolabehere and Schaffner 2013) as well as the author's original modules on the 2010 and 2011 Cooperative Congressional Election Studies. Legislator positions are Poole and Rosenthal's DW-NOMINATE scores from www.voteview.com.

Note: Unites are legislator-states. The dependent variable is legislator ideological position. μ = mean preferences of each income group by income in each state; L = low-income constituents; ML = medium-low-income constituents; H = high-income constituents; ρ = proportion of the population in each group.

*$p < .1$; **$p < .05$; ***$p < .01$

Figure 1. Relationship Between High-Income Preferences and Legislator Position

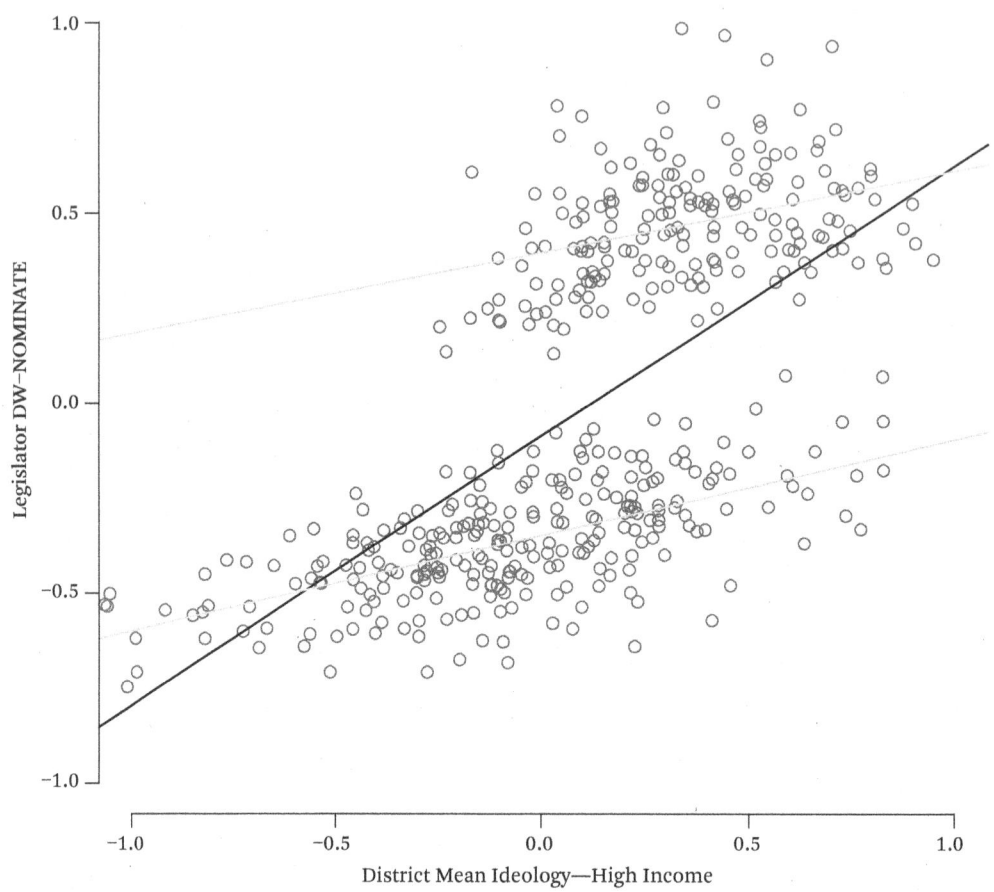

Source: Author's calculations based on the 2000 and 2004 National Annenberg Election Surveys (Annenberg Public Policy Center 2000 and 2004) and the 2006, 2008, 2010, and 2012 Cooperative Congressional Election Studies (Ansolabehere 2010a, 2010b, 2012; Ansolabehere and Schaffner 2013) as well as the author's original modules on the 2010 and 2011 Cooperative Congressional Election Studies. Legislator positions are Poole and Rosenthal's DW-NOMINATE scores from www.voteview.com.

larization in legislator positions means that the transition between liberal and conservative legislators is not smooth. In contrast, the positions of high-income constituents are spread relatively smoothly throughout the preference space. The bottom line here is that most of the variance, and hence most of the variance explained, is between-party. Within-party the lines are relatively flat and the variance explained is much less.

Figure 2 shows the univariate regression line, scatterplot, and associated within-party regression lines when the positions of low-income constituents within districts are used as the explanatory variable. There are two main differences between this plot and the previous one. First of all, the variance explained is lower, both within- and between-party, while the slope of the lines is much steeper. At the same time, the reason for this steeper slope is quite apparent: there is much less variation in terms of positions. Low-income voters are to the left of high-income voters on average, but their estimated positions also tend to be closer to zero. We might expect to find this result if poorer constituents report their policy views with greater error.

Finally, figure 3 shows what happens when

Figure 2. Relationship Between Low-Income Preferences and Legislator Position

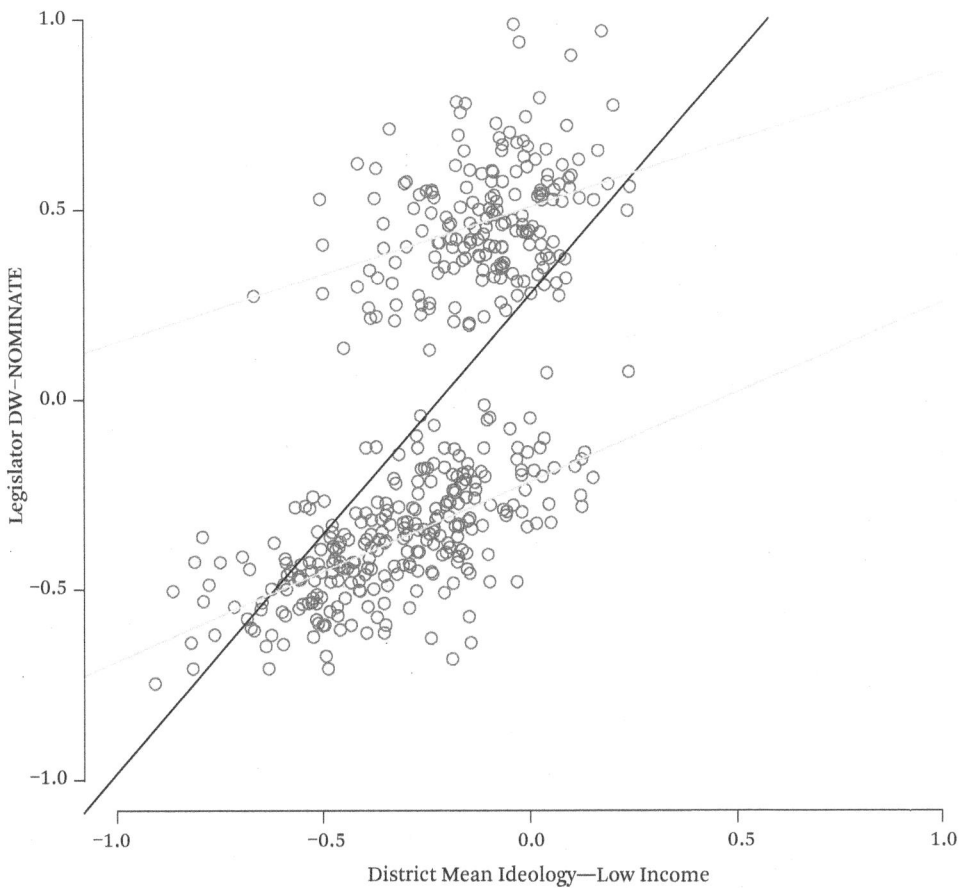

Source: Author's calculations based on the 2000 and 2004 National Annenberg Election Surveys (Annenberg Public Policy Center 2000 and 2004) and the 2006, 2008, 2010, and 2012 Cooperative Congressional Election Studies (Ansolabehere 2010a, 2010b, 2012; Ansolabehere and Schaffner 2013) as well as the author's original modules on the 2010 and 2011 Cooperative Congressional Election Studies. Legislator positions are Poole and Rosenthal's DW-NOMINATE scores from www.voteview.com.

we use the mean for the entire district to explain legislator positions. This variable explains more variance than either of the other two, with an R-squared statistic of 0.51. And yet the key feature of the relationship remains: the variance explained is mostly between-party (not too surprising, since the y variable has not changed), and our ability to explain within-party variance is relatively poor. In fact, figures 1, 2, and 3 are surprisingly similar. The differences in the relationship are overshadowed by the common disjuncture between the distribution of district opinion and the distribution of legislator positions.

One way to think about the substantive implications of these different relationships is to consider a hypothetical in which legislators do in fact respond only to low-income constituents or only to high-income constituents. We can estimate a univariate model within-party for each group, generate predicted values, and examine which set of predicted values better matches reality. Figure 4 shows the result of this exercise for the House of Representatives, including the distribution of actual legislator positions. The distributions of predicted values in figure 4 are less dispersed than the actual distribution of legislator positions. In con-

Figure 3. Relationship Between Mean District Preferences and Legislator Position

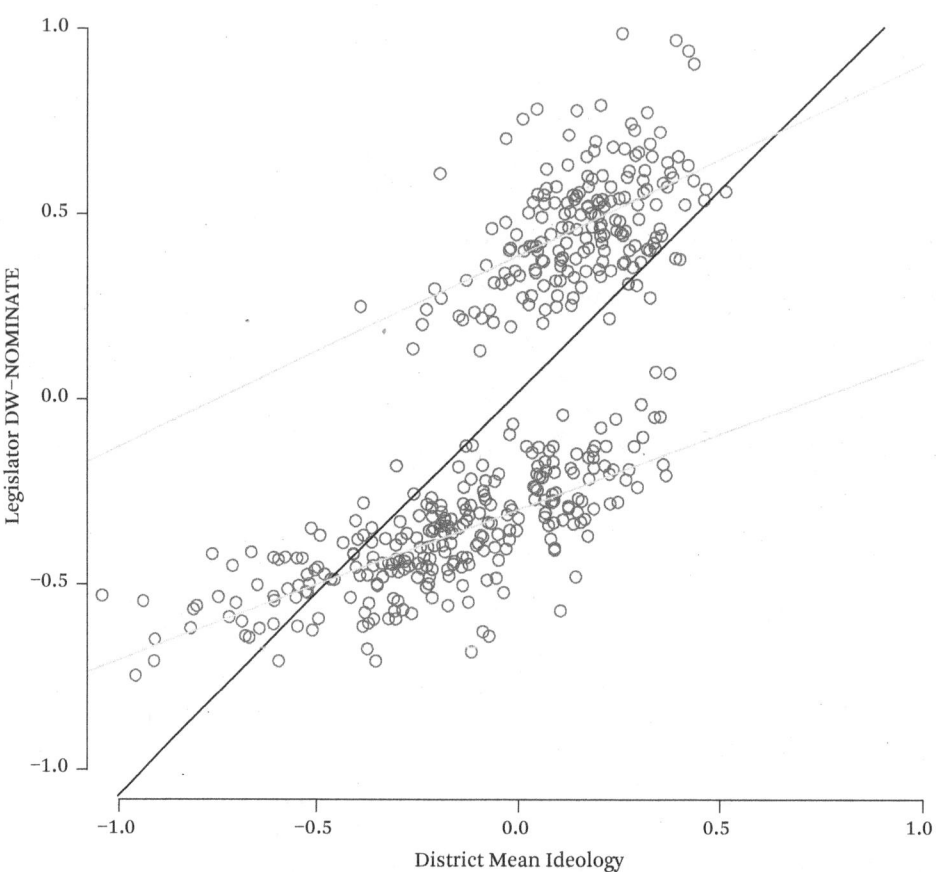

Source: Author's calculations based on the 2000 and 2004 National Annenberg Election Surveys (Annenberg Public Policy Center 2000 and 2004) and the 2006, 2008, 2010, and 2012 Cooperative Congressional Election Studies (Ansolabehere 2010a, 2010b, 2012; Ansolabehere and Schaffner 2013) as well as the author's original modules on the 2010 and 2011 Cooperative Congressional Election Studies. Legislator positions are Poole and Rosenthal's DW-NOMINATE scores from www.voteview.com.

trast, they differ little from each other. This is evidence that noisy representation of all groups is much more significant than differences in representation between people at different income levels. The disparity between the two sets of predictions is hardly noticeable.

Although this discussion of the role of the distribution of preferences has focused on the House of Representatives, these conclusions apply to the Senate as well, since it also is highly polarized. District mean preferences are a better predictor of legislator positions than the mean for high-income constituents, which is better than the mean for low-income constituents. These results hold within and across parties. Explanatory power within-party never exceeds an R-squared of 0.36.

RESULTS: INCOME AND LEGISLATOR PARTISANSHIP

Figures 1, 2, and 3 show that our ability to explain within-party variation in legislator positions using constituent ideology is limited in the U.S. House. As a result, we might think that a more reasonable model of representation is one in which constituent ideology is responsible for the party of the representative but not the representative's particular set of policy po-

Figure 4. Predicted Positions for Representation of the Rich and the Poor

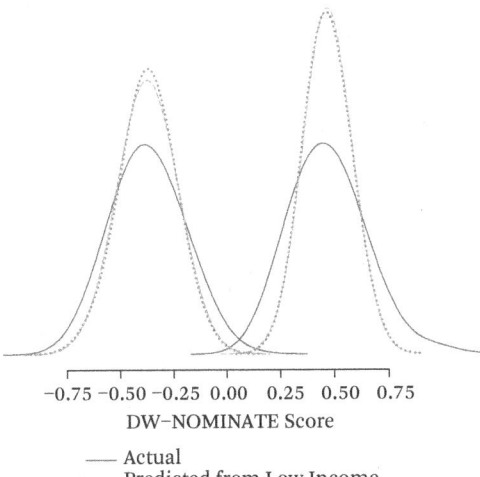

Source: Author's calculations based on the 2000 and 2004 National Annenberg Election Surveys (Annenberg Public Policy Center 2000 and 2004) and the 2006, 2008, 2010, and 2012 Cooperative Congressional Election Studies (Ansolabehere 2010a, 2010b, 2012; Ansolabehere and Schaffner 2013) as well as the author's original modules on the 2010 and 2011 Cooperative Congressional Election Studies. Legislator positions are Poole and Rosenthal's DW-NOMINATE scores from www.voteview.com.

sitions. For our purposes, the question becomes: are high-income people more important in deciding the party of the representative than low-income people?

To test this hypothesis, I adapt the regression models from table 5. Instead of using a linear model in which the dependent variable is the legislator's position or DW-NOMINATE score, I employ a logistic regression model in which the dependent variable is whether or not the legislator is a Democrat. Districts or states are more likely to be represented by Democrats when the population is more liberal. However, if higher-income people have more importance in determining electoral outcomes, we might expect the preferences of higher-income people to be a more important determinant of the partisanship of representatives.

Table 6 reports the result of a logistic regression model along the same lines as table 5, but using the Senate and with the party of the legislator as the dependent variable. Models 1 and 2 suggest that in states with more conservative citizens, either low-income or high-income, the senator representing that state is less likely to be a Democrat. Model 3 shows that when these income groups are included in the same model, the coefficients for the top three income groups indicate that conservative views lead to less likelihood of Democratic representation. However, the coefficient for the poor is insignificant and substantially in the wrong direction. The greatest coefficient is for the views of high-income constituents, although this difference is not significant. The coefficient on the proportion poor suggests that poorer states are more likely to be represented by Democratic senators, all else equal. These coefficients are unstable across different sessions of the Senate, but the coefficient for the highest-income group is always the greatest in magnitude.

Table 7 repeats this model specification for the House of Representatives. The first two columns of the table show findings similar to those in table 5. In a model including only the preferences of low-income constituents, the slope of the relationship between the mean preferences of low-income constituents and the probability of electing a Democrat is significant. This relationship is also significant in a model with the mean preferences of high-income constituents as the primary independent variable. The slope of this relationship is significantly less steep, although the model fits somewhat better. In both cases, the relationship is negative, as expected: more conservative constituencies are less likely to elect Democrats.

The third column of Table 7 shows the model including all covariates. Although in every case the relationship between the preferences of each group and the probability of electing a Democrat has the expected sign, only two of the coefficients are significant. The positions of high-income people have by far the largest slope. The medium-high-income group appears to have the smallest slope, while the low-income and medium-low-income groups are in a close tie for second place. The coefficient on the preferences of the rich is signifi-

Table 6. Logistic Regressions Explaining Legislator Party in the U.S. Senate (1 = Democrat)

	Legislator Party		
	(1)	(2)	(3)
μ_L	−6.91***		
	(2.41)		
μ_H		−6.21***	
		(1.50)	
ρ_H	−4.72	−6.10	−14.18
	(20.55)	(22.56)	(24.63)
ρ_L	18.64	33.89**	28.58*
	(12.86)	(14.72)	(15.47)
ρ_{ML}	−30.33	−45.18	−52.17
	(25.18)	(28.83)	(32.21)
$\rho_H \times \mu_H$			−29.54*
			(15.94)
$\rho_{MH} \times \mu_{MH}$			−7.83
			(12.34)
$\rho_{ML} \times \mu_{ML}$			−9.91
			(14.83)
$\rho_L \times \mu_L$			14.80
			(20.30)
Constant	4.52	8.03	12.74
	(11.40)	(12.13)	(13.51)
Observations	106	106	106
Log likelihood	−58.66	−51.92	−50.14
Akaike information criterion	127.32	113.84	116.28

Source: Author's calculations based on the 2000 and 2004 National Annenberg Election Surveys (Annenberg Public Policy Center 2000 and 2004) and the 2006, 2008, 2010, and 2012 Cooperative Congressional Election Studies (Ansolabehere 2010a, 2010b, 2012; Ansolabehere and Schaffner 2013) as well as the author's original modules on the 2010 and 2011 Cooperative Congressional Election Studies. Legislator positions are Poole and Rosenthal's DW-NOMINATE scores from www.voteview.com.

Note: Unites are legislator-states. The dependent variable is legislator party. μ = mean preferences of each income group by income in each state; L = low-income constituents; ML = medium-low-income constituents; H = high-income constituents; ρ = proportion of the population in each group.

*$p < .1$; **$p < .05$; ***$p < .01$

Table 7. Logistic Regressions Explaining Legislator Party in the U.S. House of Representatives (1 = Democrat)

	Legislator Party		
	(1)	(2)	(3)
μ_L	−7.81*** (0.83)		
μ_H		−5.24*** (0.53)	
ρ_H	−1.17 (4.67)	−2.66 (4.85)	−4.03 (5.64)
ρ_L	13.72*** (3.98)	15.00*** (4.20)	10.91** (4.51)
ρ_{ML}	−4.24 (6.05)	−6.17 (6.40)	−1.59 (7.10)
$\rho_H \times \mu_H$			−19.68*** (4.75)
$\rho_{MH} \times \mu_{MH}$			−4.55 (3.09)
$\rho_{ML} \times \mu_{ML}$			−8.71** (4.14)
$\rho_L \times \mu_L$			−9.71* (5.53)
Constant	−2.64 (2.64)	0.32 (2.73)	−0.60 (3.14)
Observations	445	445	445
Log likelihood	−218.33	−202.27	−180.35
Akaike information criterion	446.67	414.53	376.71

Source: Author's calculations based on the 2000 and 2004 National Annenberg Election Surveys (Annenberg Public Policy Center 2000 and 2004) and the 2006, 2008, 2010, and 2012 Cooperative Congressional Election Studies (Ansolabehere 2010a, 2010b, 2012; Ansolabehere and Schaffner 2013) as well as the author's original modules on the 2010 and 2011 Cooperative Congressional Election Studies. Legislator positions are Poole and Rosenthal's DW-NOMINATE scores from www.voteview.com.

Note: Unites are legislator-states. The dependent variable is legislator party. μ = mean preferences of each income group by income in each state; L = low-income constituents; ML = medium-low-income constituents; H = high-income constituents; ρ = proportion of the population in each group.
*$p < .1$; **$p < .05$; ***$p < .01$

Figure 5. Probability of a Democratic Legislator by Ideology of Income Groups

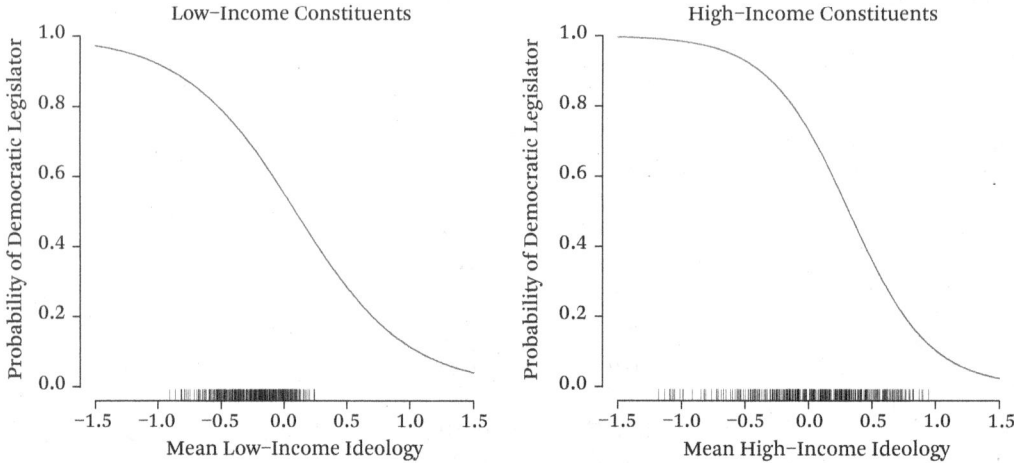

Source: Author's calculations based on the 2000 and 2004 National Annenberg Election Surveys (Annenberg Public Policy Center 2000 and 2004) and the 2006, 2008, 2010, and 2012 Cooperative Congressional Election Studies (Ansolabehere 2010a, 2010b, 2012; Ansolabehere and Schaffner 2013) as well as the author's original modules on the 2010 and 2011 Cooperative Congressional Election Studies. Legislator positions are Poole and Rosenthal's DW-NOMINATE scores from www.voteview.com.
Note: This figure comes from a model very similar to the one in column 3 of table 7, but with all direct effects included. Probabilities are calculated with all variables except the one on the x-axis held fixed at their mean. The tick marks on the bottom of the graph show the distribution of the actual x values.

cantly greater than the coefficients on the preferences of the other groups, which are all statistically indistinguishable. However, this result does not hold in the 106th or 107th Congresses. Notably, in all specifications, and in all sessions of Congress, the proportion of the district that is poor has a substantial positive effect on the probability of electing a Democrat.

Coefficients are notoriously difficult to interpret in logistic regression models. A visualization is helpful in understanding the substantive difference between the effects for the rich and the poor. I use a model very similar to the one from the last column of table 7 to show the predicted change in the probability of electing a Democrat based on a change in the ideology of the mean low-income and high-income constituent, respectively. The only difference between the model used to calculate these probabilites and the model in table 7 is that the former includes all direct effects, following the folk wisdom on using interactions in regression models (Brambor, Clark, and Golder 2006). This change in specification makes very little difference in the resulting probabilities. To calculate the change in probability I hold all other variables besides the variable of interest at their mean.

Figure 5 shows the result of this exercise for the House of Representatives. The left panel shows the predicted probability of a Democratic legislator given the preferences of low-income constituents, and the right panel shows the predicted probability of a Democratic legislator given the preferences of high-income constituents. As expected from the regression table, the slope is steeper for high-income constituents. Nonetheless, the slope in the left panel is not flat: Democratic legislators are substantially more likely when poor constituents are liberal than when they are conservative. Note that if we were to examine the 106th or 107th Congresses, the slopes for the preferences of the higher-income group would be flatter, reversing this relationship.

The "rug" for each graph shows the distribution of the mean constituent preferences. As discussed, the variation in preferences is substantially greater for high-income than low-income constituents. In this case, the range where the slope for high-income constituents exceeds the slope for low-income constituents occurs in a region where there are no data for low-income constituents. Specifically, there are very few districts where the mean ideology of low-income constituents is to the right of zero. In contrast, for high-income constituents, most of the decline in the likelihood of electing a Democrat occurs to the right of zero. Our analysis has told us that the slope is steeper in the right panel, but this steep slope occurs in a region where we have no data in the left panel. In other words, we cannot tell how unlikely the election of a Democrat would be in a district with very conservative poor residents because no such district exists.

CONCLUSION

In this paper, I have shown that while there is some evidence that lower-income people are less represented in Congress, this evidence is robust only in the context of the Senate, not the House of Representatives. Even in the Senate, the substantive importance of this difference is limited in comparison to the gap in overall representation. Given the small extent of differential representation and the uncertainty regarding it, priority should be given to understanding overall representation and the reasons why the distribution of legislator preferences is so different from the distribution of average preferences in districts. Separating the public into large categories by income does not seem to help us solve this puzzle.

To understand how representation is unequal, better theories of representation are needed. A good theory of representation should account for the fact that most of the variance in legislative positions is currently between parties. With such a theory, political scientists would be better able to evaluate whether legislators take the preferences of their constituents into account without regard to income. In this paper, I have used two very basic theories: that legislators represent the mean voter, and that the party of the legislator is determined by the mean voter. Future research should strive to build richer theories of representation from microfoundations.

One possible explanation for the small amount of differential representation that I find is that there is more measurement error in the preferences of the poor than in those of the rich. This would affect the analyis insofar as preferences have been imperfectly observed. However, legislators as well as political scientists may have more difficulty observing these preferences. Future research should investigate this possibility as a cause of the weak representational link.

There is one argument that I have not made in this paper: that low-income people are in fact well represented. Work that makes the argument that the political system does not represent the poor very well may be right. Much depends on a value judgment about what aspect of preferences should be represented. Certainly the political system has not responded to the economic needs of lower-income people in a way that standard political economy models would predict (Bonica et al. 2013; Hacker and Pierson 2011). The findings of this paper may plausibly answer the question posed by Adam Bonica and his colleagues (2013): why hasn't democracy slowed rising inequality? If legislators respond only weakly to their constituents in general—and *perhaps* respond especially weakly to their low-income constituents in particular—then not one but two conditions are violated that would be needed to beget a democratic response to rising inequality. Determining which institutions might affect both of these links and examining the downstream effects of doing so are urgent matters for future research.

REFERENCES

Achen, Christopher H., and Larry M. Bartels. 2012. "Blind Retrospection: Why Shark Attacks Are Bad for Democracy." Working paper. Nashville, TN: Vanderbilt University, Center for the Study of Democratic Institutions.

The Annenberg Public Policy Center at the University of Pennsylvania. 2000. "2000 National Annenberg Election Survey." http://www.annenbergpublicpolicycenter.org/political-communication/naes/ (accessed May 25, 2016).

———. 2004. "2004 National Annenberg Election Survey." http://www.annenbergpublicpolicycenter.org/political-communication/naes/ (accessed May 25, 2016).

Ansolabehere, Stephen. 2010a. "CCES, Common

Content, 2006." Harvard Dataverse, V4. http://hdl.handle.net/1902.1/14002 (accessed May 25, 2016).

———. 2010b. "CCES, Common Content, 2008." Harvard Dataverse, V6. http://hdl.handle.net/1902.1/14003 (accessed May 25, 2016).

———. 2012. "CCES, Common Content, 2010." Harvard Dataverse, V3. http://hdl.handle.net/1902.1/17705 (accessed May 25, 2016).

Ansolabehere, Stephen, Jonathan Rodden, and James M. Snyder. 2008. "The Strength of Issues: Using Multiple Measures to Gauge Preference Stability, Ideological Constraint, and Issue Voting." *American Political Science Review* 102(2): 215–32.

Ansolabehere, Stephen, Brian Schaffner. 2013. "CCES Common Content, 2012." Harvard Dataverse, V8. http://hdl.handle.net/1902.1/21447 (accessed May 25, 2016).

Bartels, Larry M. 2009. *Unequal Democracy: The Political Economy of the New Gilded Age*. Princeton, N.J.: Princeton University Press.

Bhatti, Yosef, and Robert S. Erikson. 2011. "How Poorly Are the Poor Represented in the U.S. Senate?" In *Who Gets Represented?* edited by Peter K. Enns and Christopher Wlezien. New York: Russell Sage Foundation.

Black, Duncan. 1948. "On the Rationale of Group Decision-Making." *Journal of Political Economy* 56(1): 23–34.

Bonica, Adam, Nolan McCarty, Keith T. Poole, and Howard Rosenthal. 2013. "Why Hasn't Democracy Slowed Rising Inequality?" *Journal of Economic Perspectives* 27(3): 103–23.

Brambor, Thomas, William Roberts Clark, and Matt Golder. 2006. "Understanding Interaction Models: Improving Empirical Analyses." *Political Analysis* 14(1): 63–82.

Brunner, Eric, Stephen L. Ross, and Ebonya Washington. 2013. "Does Less Income Mean Less Representation?" *American Economic Journal: Economic Policy* 5(2): 53–76.

Butler, Daniel M. 2014. *Representing the Advantaged: How Politicians Reinforce Inequality*. New York: Cambridge University Press.

Campbell, Angus, Philip E. Converse, Warren E. Miller, and Donald E. Stokes. 1966. *The American Voter*. New York: Wiley.

Caplin, Andrew, and Barry Nalebuff. 1991. "Aggregation and Social Choice: A Mean Voter Theorem." *Econometrica: Journal of the Econometric Society* 59(1): 1–23.

Clinton, Joshua D. 2006. "Representation in Congress: Constituents and Roll Calls in the 106th House." *Journal of Politics* 68(2): 397–409.

Clinton, Joshua, Simon Jackman, and Douglas Rivers. 2004. "The Statistical Analysis of Roll Call Data." *American Political Science Review* 98(2): 355–70.

Downs, Anthony. 1957. "An Economic Theory of Political Action in a Democracy." *Journal of Political Economy* 65(2): 135–50.

Fiorina, Morris P., and Samuel J. Abrams. 2012. *Disconnect: The Breakdown of Representation in American Politics*. Vol. 11. Norman: University of Oklahoma Press.

Gilens, Martin. 2012. *Affluence and Influence: Economic Inequality and Political Power in America*. Princeton, N.J.: Princeton University Press.

Gilens, Martin, and Benjamin I. Page. 2014. "Testing Theories of American Politics: Elites, Interest Groups, and Average Citizens." *Perspectives on Politics* 12(3): 564–81. doi: 10.1017/S1537592714001595.

Hacker, Jacob S., and Paul Pierson. 2011. *Winner-Take-All Politics: How Washington Made the Rich Richer—and Turned Its Back on the Middle Class*. New York: Simon & Schuster.

Hill, Seth J., and Chris Tausanovitch. 2015. "A Disconnect in Representation? Comparison of Trends in Congressional and Public Polarization." *Journal of Politics* 77(4): 1058–75.

Lewis, Jeffrey B., and Chris Tausanovitch. 2013. "Has Joint Scaling Solved the Achen Objection to Miller and Stokes?" Working paper. Los Angeles: University of California, Department of Political Science.

Poole, Keith T., and Howard Rosenthal. 1997. *Congress: A Political-Economic History of Roll Call Voting*. New York: Oxford University Press.

Schofield, Norman. 2007. "The Mean Voter Theorem: Necessary and Sufficient Conditions for Convergent Equilibrium." *Review of Economic Studies* 74(3): 965–80.

Tausanovitch, Chris, and Christopher Warshaw. 2013. "Measuring Constituent Policy Preferences in Congress, State Legislatures, and Cities." *Journal of Politics* 75(2): 330–42.

———. 2014. "Do Legislator Positions Affect Constituent Voting Decisions in U.S. House Elections?" Unpublished paper. University of California, Los Angeles, and Massachusetts Institute of Technology, Cambridge, Mass.

Zaller, John. 1992. *The Nature and Origins of Mass Opinion*. New York: Cambridge University Press.

Shining the Light on Dark Money: Political Spending by Nonprofits

DREW DIMMERY AND ANDREW PETERSON

The past decade has seen an increase in public attention on the role of campaign donations and outside spending. This has led some donors to seek ways of skirting disclosure requirements, such as by contributing through nonprofits that allow for greater privacy. These nonprofits nonetheless clearly aim to influence policy discussions and have a direct impact, in some cases, on electoral outcomes. We develop a technique for identifying nonprofits engaged in political activity that relies not on their formal disclosure, which is often understated or omitted, but on text analysis of their websites. We generate political activity scores for 339,818 organizations and validate our measure through crowdsourcing. Using our measure, we characterize the number and distribution of political nonprofits and estimate how much these groups spend for political purposes.

Keywords: nonprofits, dark money, outside lobbying, transparency

While political science has focused much of its attention on campaign contributions by political action committees (PACs), recent spending on politically related activity by nonprofits may be greater in magnitude. For example, in 2012 the Planned Parenthood Action Fund, a nonprofit advocacy group, spent twice as much as Planned Parenthood Votes, its PAC counterpart, in the entire 2012 cycle (Planned Parenthood Federation of America 2012). Similar examples can be found across the political spectrum. Although nonprofit organizations—groups organized under section 501(c) of the U.S. Code—are subject to limits on their political activity, many spend significant amounts of money to promote their political opinions. Anecdotal and journalistic evidence suggests that in the last few years a growing number of donors with political aims have begun channeling donations through nonprofits in lieu of, or in addition to, direct contributions to candidates or PACs. Since donors to nonprofits need not be disclosed, some have referred to this channel of influence as "dark money." Failing to observe these cash flows threatens the validity of research on special-interest politics.

Formal studies have not been conducted, but there is good reason to think that nonprofits do not adequately disclose their political activities. Evidence from related activities such as lobbying and campaign contributions suggests that political actors often disclose the minimum allowable by law and may even introduce errors into their reports to make trans-

Drew Dimmery is a doctoral candidate in the Department of Politics at New York University. **Andrew Peterson** is a doctoral candidate in the Department of Politics at New York University.

The authors would like to thank the participants in the Russell Sage Foundation "Big Data in Political Economy" conference and two anonymous reviewers for their comments. This research was made possible by funding support from the New York University George Downs Prize. Direct correspondence to: Drew Dimmery at drew@drewdimmery.com, Department of Politics, Second Floor, 19 W 4th St., New York, NY 10012; and Andrew Peterson at ajp502@nyu.edu, Department of Politics, Second Floor, 19 W 4th St., New York, NY 10012.

parency more difficult (LaPira and Thomas 2014). Legal requirements to disclose vary by the type of activity and the type of nonprofit, and in many cases they are not very strict. The vast majority of nonprofits do not need to disclose their donors, and approval procedures have often been pro forma. In 2013 the Internal Revenue Service (IRS) became concerned about the political activities of nonprofits and sought to initiate reviews, but the agency lacked an effective means of identifying which organizations to review among the many thousands. Its approach generated a scandal when it targeted political nonprofits using key words (like "tea party") in organizations' names (Drawbaugh and Dixon 2014).

Whether or not a nonprofit was originally created with the intention of engaging in political activity, it may over time develop political aims. Since many nonprofits aim to shape the world toward their conception of the common good or the good of their members, it is only natural that at some point they would consider political means of doing so, whether to further their goals or simply to protect themselves against possible political threats. Recently a number of such activities have been documented illustrating the increasing role played by nonprofits in politics. For example, in the 2012 campaign more than $300 million in dark money was spent by nonprofits directly aimed at political campaigns, despite not legally being identified as such (Maguire 2014a). The overall trend suggests that spending by such groups has grown much more rapidly than other forms of political spending in the past decade (Maguire 2014b). New forms of funding for nonprofits have even included foreign governments specifically trying to influence U.S. policy outcomes through their 501(c) grantees. Unlike a lobbyist acting on behalf of foreign entities, these nonprofits do not have to register their funding source (Lipton 2014).

Understanding the role played by such undisclosed funding is naturally difficult since it is not obvious how to identify the relevant actors. Using machine learning algorithms and text analysis, we identify which groups engage in political advocacy. This is challenging insofar as many groups seek to obfuscate or understate the extent to which they operate in a partisan or political manner. Out of 339,818 nonprofits that filed in 2012, we identify those with a political focus by using information released by the IRS as well as a new data set we collected of text scraped from the website of each organization. Although we presume that political organizations strategically choose the text content of their websites, we also presume that our text-mining algorithm can identify subtle clues that nonetheless classify political organizations as such. By calibrating against a subset of known political organizations, we are able to pick up the features that correspond to political activity. We then validate this claim through crowdsourcing: we have independent third-party coders identify whether a random sample of organizations are political.

This analysis allows us to estimate interesting quantities relevant to the U.S. political landscape, such as the aggregate political activity by these statutorily nonpartisan organizations. We present an array of descriptive analyses of these organizations across issue area, type, and geographical location and, given assumptions about general trends, provide estimates of politically adjusted revenue (PAR)—the part of nonprofits' revenue that is devoted to political activity. Such a comprehensive analysis of the political behavior of nonprofits has not to our knowledge been attempted. Our results suggest that even a conservative approach to estimating the value of nonprofit political activity shows it to be quite substantial. Future research should examine the role of this spending in special-interest politics and in political mobilization.

POLITICAL ACTIVITY BY NONPROFITS

Not surprisingly, given that the role of nonprofits in campaigns has been identified as significant only recently, the existing academic literature does not address the political role of nonprofits directly.[1] There is naturally considerable scholarship on the role of money in political campaigns and the strategies and actors

---

1. For one recent paper that does address the role of nonprofits, specifically in relation to climate change, see Ramey and Rothenberg (n.d.).

involved in generating such funds. In this section, we review some of the reasons why nonprofits play a unique role in political campaigns and issue advocacy, starting from the fact that nonprofits face different disclosure requirements. We also review anecdotal accounts of actors strategically using nonprofits to avoid disclosure, and we consider the possible relationship to political polarization as well as the broad ways in which nonprofits may engage in political work beyond federal election campaigns.

An obvious concern about the role of money in politics is whether it inhibits fair competition or simply allows political actors to express their views. Empirical studies using variation in state laws suggests that the public is interested in passing such rules because contribution limits may indeed promote competitiveness (Stratmann 2010). To the extent that competing parties or interest groups stand to benefit or gain differentially from such regulations, however, it is natural that political actors would seek to influence such rules.[2] Indeed, the new role played by nonprofits is only one of the latest ways in which the U.S. political landscape has been transformed by the introduction of new forms of giving and spending. Attempts to regulate campaign spending began in the United States in the late nineteenth and early twentieth centuries but only took hold in 1972 with the enactment of the Federal Election Campaign Act of 1971. These rules have been modified repeatedly, including by Congress, the courts, and the Federal Election Commission (FEC). In 1979, for example, the FEC opened the door to "soft money"—money that is not given to an individual federal candidate and for which restrictions on donation size are relaxed.

Another approach to campaign finance involves reporting requirements rather than limits on spending. Such disclosure requirements are important because they may affect voters' perceptions. A study of soft money and issue advocacy found that voters are not well informed about who is responsible when this money is used to fund advertisements and that being given this information changes their reaction to the advertisement and the election (Magleby and Monson 2004). This suggests that the issue of whether donors are disclosed is substantively important, and indeed the difference between disclosing and nondisclosing groups has recently become part of the public debate. With respect to the political role of nonprofits, most 501(c) organizations are not required to disclose their donors.[3] These organizations consist of everything from hospitals to universities to labor unions to think tanks. The Supreme Court ruled in 1958 in favor of such protections of anonymity in *NAACP v. Alabama* because individuals might fear that disclosure of their political beliefs would lead to personal reprisals.[4]

More recently, this protection has been used by nonprofits to avoid transparency laws adopted as part of the Bipartisan Campaign Reform Act of 2002. Crossroads GPS, a conservative 501(c)(4) organization, for example, spent $190 million overall as reported to the IRS in 2012, but reported to the FEC that only around $70 million of that was election-related spending (Edsall 2014). The FEC does not require that "educational" activities, or activities meant to "persuade," be reported, nor does it put any limits on this spending. The role of such spending, conceptualized as "outside lobbying" by Ken Kollman (1998) to reflect its relationship to attempts to influence Congress directly, may be to mobilize group members, to reveal high levels of public support for a measure, or to act as a costly signal. To evaluate such theories, the spending must be observed, but nonprofit organizations may be missed by approaches relying on FEC data or surveys.

Observing this spending is also important to understanding how campaign money contributes to or ameliorates political polarization. Insofar as donors are making a strategic choice to contribute either anonymously or

---

2. For evidence suggesting that firms do not benefit from soft-money contributions, see Ansolabehere et al. (2004).

3. Only 501(c)(3) private foundations are required to disclose their donors.

4. *National Association for the Advancement of Colored People v. Alabama*, 357 U.S. 449 (1958).

publicly, we should not expect that the subset who make public contributions will be representative of all donors. Although it is clear that a significant amount of money is funneled toward indirect public advocacy, there is no systematic way to measure this activity at this time.

Our estimates of the politicality of nonprofits allow us to compare total nonprofit income by type and geographic region. Although nonprofits have been spending money for political purposes for decades, they spent less than $15 million per cycle until 2008, according to the Center for Responsive Politics (CRP). In the 2008 cycle, nonprofits expanded their involvement in "issue advocacy," which avoids being labeled as electioneering by carefully avoiding any reference to specific candidates (even when advocacy for a certain perspective on an issue clearly favors one candidate over another). By the CRP's estimate, in the 2008 cycle nonprofit spending jumped to more than $70 million, and then to almost $300 million in 2012 (Maguire 2014a). Of course, restrictions are placed on nonprofits' engagement in political behavior, but the boundary between what is allowed and what is not is unclear and being expanded. Enforcement of these rules is also an issue since the FEC, comprising equal numbers of Democratic and Republican members, has been deadlocked over rulings on constraints on political activity.[5]

DATA AND METHODS

The first step in identifying political nonprofits is specifying how "political" will be defined, but establishing a comprehensive definition is beyond the scope of this paper. The question has been a concern of political philosophy from at least Confucius and Plato up to contemporary debates about feminism, liberalism, and communitarianism. Since we are primarily concerned with issue advocacy and electioneering, our working definition is based on Supreme Court rulings and the FEC requirements for disclosure, and it focuses on specific observable characteristics related to political activities.

In particular, electioneering advertisement has been defined in *Buckley v. Valeo* as relying on the so-called magic words test: "express advocacy" is relevant to the FEC only if it uses particular phrases such as "vote for."[6] References to individual candidates thus do not imply that speech falls into the more heavily regulated category of express advocacy. We broaden this definition to include all references to a current political office-holder or candidate. This is important since we are directly looking for the kind of deregulated political speech that tends to fall under the broad auspices of "issue advocacy" wherein political issues and candidates are discussed, but without explicit calls for support through the "magic words" of post-*Buckley* express advocacy. As such, we must include a nonprofit as political if it makes reference to proposed or current legislation or regulation if we are to pick up this kind of issue advocacy.

Finally, we include the most strictly regulated form of speech—that which expressly promotes or opposes political candidates or policies. In essence, this final category picks up what is regulated by the FEC as "political" under current law. Thus, our definition is wider in scope than current law insomuch as it includes electioneering and issue advocacy (in addition to simple express advocacy).

The main methodological goal of this project is to identify 501(c) organizations that are political. Since there is no comprehensive method for attaining a list of the agendas of every nonprofit organization in the United States, we rely on an approach that imputes the politicality of organizations through their descriptions of themselves online. This approach grows out of a substantial literature on the scaling of political texts but is novel owing to the unique challenges of this environment (Grimmer and Stewart 2013).

Unfortunately, we do not have a simple sampling frame of texts to use. There are no well-defined manifestos for each organization, nor does every organization have a simple corpus of writings and publications. To address this problem, we rely on a novel method of collect-

---

5. For an earlier example of such deadlock, see Salant (2009). For a recent example, see Gold (2013).

6. *James L. Buckley, et al. v. Francis R. Valeo, Secretary of the United States Senate, et al.*, 424 U.S. 1 (1976).

ing texts to use. Vast quantities of text are available on the Internet about the majority of the organizations in our study population. Our goal is to gain a rich set of texts on which to ground an analysis by matching organizations with their web pages. This matching task is difficult, however, since there are no comprehensive listings of the web presence of nonprofit organizations. We use the Yahoo! BOSS Search API to rapidly perform a query for the name of each organization in our data set and retrieve the fifty best URL results, in JSON format. We then scrape the web text at these URLs and clean the HTML using Beautiful Soup in Python. In general, we use only the top result, but when this is unavailable, we use the second-best result.

Classifiers are machine learning algorithms that seek to distinguish between two or more classes (in our case, political/nonpolitical). These algorithms take a set of data with ex ante "labels" indicating class membership and learn how best to use other "features" of the data (such as words) to predict these classes. Since we do not have clean training labels (categorizations as political or not) for even a subset of organizations, our labels are almost certainly measured with error, even though we take a supervised learning approach. We adopt two methods to create labels, both of which frequently label political groups as nonpolitical. The first method is simply to examine the names of organizations and label them as political when they include one of a set of keywords.[7] This approach is very basic, but it provides a good number of effective matches. Moreover, this approach reflects the controversial method used by the IRS to target groups (predominantly conservative, according to critics) for audits of political activity. This approach gives us 3,255 groups labeled as political, with the remainder tentatively labeled as nonpolitical.

Our second labeling scheme is to use responses to questions asked by the IRS on the tax returns of nonprofits (made available to the public by the IRS). These questions are binary choices as to whether they influence legislation, engage in propaganda, or try to influence public elections. These criteria are incomplete, however, since political nonprofits do much of their political work through direct issue advocacy, which need not be reported to the IRS. That is, only organizations rated as political according to our third criterion would be included in this scheme. Probably the lion's share of political nonprofits answer "no" to these questions. Nevertheless, this approach provides us with 8,343 labeled political organizations. In addition, we collect the web pages of the full population of 10,921 political action committees registered with the FEC and label each of these as political to supplement our training data with groups known to be political.

Altogether, we have 435,495 groups in our sample for which we have names and employer identification numbers. Of these groups, we identify 339,818 groups with valid websites.[8] Our approach is based on the assumption that groups with website text similar to that of groups labeled political are likely to be political. By adjusting the penalty associated with making certain types of error, we embed knowledge about the direction of errors in our classifier. In other words, we embed an expectation that organizations labeled as nonpolitical are much more likely to be political than organizations labeled as political are likely to be nonpolitical. Thus, our algorithm will produce a range of scores that assign some probability of being political to nonpolitical groups but are more likely to uncover political groups that would otherwise go unidentified. We weight each class of labels (political/nonpolitical) by the inverse of their ubiquity in the initial data. Thus, we take an organization's use on its website of language similar to that of a known political organization as a strong signal that it should be properly classified as political.

---

7. We use the following stems as keywords: "action fund," "advoca," "politic," "republican," "democrat," "conservativ," "liberal," "libertar," "socialis," "communis," "constitution," "whig," "federalis," "freedom," "liberty," "government," "progressiv," "feminis," "human right," "public interest," and "national secur."

8. Some smaller organizations have no independent web presence, and thus search results return only third-party websites that republish the data provided in bulk by the IRS.

It is useful for understanding our contribution to compare our approach to how the Center for Responsive Politics imputes the politicality of nonprofits. The CRP focuses on the largest groups that disclose federal political expenditures to the FEC and then uses these groups to trace other associated nonprofits.[9] We instead develop an index of politicality based not on disclosure to government agencies but on actual public-facing behavior. There are a number of benefits to this approach. First, it provides a broader understanding of the political behavior of nonprofits by considering spending that need not always be reported to the federal government, such as spending on local or state politics, issue advocacy, turnout mobilization, and policy research. Since much of the concern surrounding dark money centers on the paucity of disclosure requirements, it is important to develop tools that do not rely on disclosure. Our machine learning approach contributes to other types of text analysis involving politicians' speeches and statements, legislation, and the news media.

To simplify, our approach seeks to understand which organizations look most like our labeled political organizations on the basis of what they say. Loading the entire corpus into computer memory is not a feasible solution for data of this size, so our model choice is guided by the availability of appropriate online machine learning algorithms, which need not be trained all in a single call but can instead be called progressively on small portions of the overall data. To compare to common methodologies used by political scientists, consider Wordscores or Correspondence Analysis, two common tools to capture latent dimensions of textlike data (Lowe 2008; Greenacre 1984). These methods cannot be divided into steps that utilize only part of the full data and then update iteratively. Instead, training must be performed all at one time. Similarly, traditional support vector machines struggle in classification problems with many observations, despite their ability to deal with high-dimensional feature representations.

Our model consists of a naive Bayes classifier trained iteratively on our labeled training data (Hastie, Tibshirani, and Friedman 2009; Rennie et al. 2003). Naive Bayes classifiers, though somewhat rudimentary, provide simple and rough means that are often sufficient for good classification (Zhang 2004). Naive Bayes provides a basic but imminently scalable solution to text classification. Mathematically, naive Bayes can be seen as a sort of linear regression in log space of labels on word frequencies.[10]

Naive Bayes is trained iteratively in minibatches of 1,000 documents in Python using Scikit-learn (Pedregosa 2011). This generates the predicted probabilities of being political for each organization, which are used prominently in the analyses to follow. Groups receive high predicted probabilities when the text of their website uses language similar to that of a group initially labeled as political. Although this is expressed as a probability, given that our initial training data are imperfect, these predictions should not be interpreted as the probability of an organization being political but rather as an index determining the similarity of its language to that of labeled political organizations. For this reason, we refer to this measure hereafter as a "probability index," or simply a "measure."

---

9. That is, the CRP begins by examining organizations that reported large political expenditures to the FEC (thereby leaving out most spending on issue advocacy, voter mobilization, and state- and local-level efforts). It then notes all grants larger than $25,000 made by or to these political nonprofits. From this, it estimates the indirect funding of politics through the grantees of organizations to provide a sense of the "attributable spending" of these groups. This methodology relies, however, on the disclosure of particular types of political money (to either the IRS or the FEC), which organizations may seek to avoid when such disclosure is not statutorily required. See OpenSecrets.org, "Political Nonprofits: Methodology," http://www.opensecrets.org/outsidespending/methodology.php (accessed August 9, 2016).

10. Words are alphabetic tokens of length 3 to 17. In our classification model, we use "Laplace smoothing," which adds a small amount (we use a value of 2) to every token's frequency count, effectively placing a prior on the informational content of very infrequent words and shrinking down their effects.

To extract a binary measurement of politicality, the next section evaluates the accuracy of the measure and derives the appropriate threshold at which to divide political from nonpolitical organizations using crowdsourcing.

VALIDATION

Having generated a measure of whether a nonprofit is likely to be political, we demonstrate that this measure is not the same as our initial training labels and further that this measure accords with what humans reading the text of the website would believe about its political content. To begin we note that, while it makes little difference whether we create our training labels using the IRS-based or the keyword/names-based approach, the fact that the politicality measure we generate is quite different from the initial training labels suggests that it adds value over a more naive approach. The correlation between our measure using IRS labels and our measure using name-based labels is 0.89, while the correlation between the training labels themselves is 0.83. These similarities end, however, when we compare the output of naive Bayes to the training labels. The correlation between training labels and our generated IRS-based measure is 0.25 (and 0.17 for the name-based measures). This means that the measures we produce using naive Bayes are indeed quite different from the initial labels, though still similar to each other. That is, our measure identifies a substantially different set of organizations than do the reporting standards under the existing regulatory regime.

To get a sense of how our naive Bayes model distinguishes between political and nonpolitical organizations we can look at the loadings on words to understand which of them provide the most leverage. The top one hundred most political and nonpolitical words for each model are presented in table 1. The most political words for both the model using name-based labels and the model based on IRS reports refer to what is clearly political in nature: for instance, partisan politics (democratic, republican, conservative, liberal), political institutions (congress, house, senate, fec), and other political actors (committees, pac, obama). Nonpolitical words refer to what is nonpolitical in nature, such as religion (church, ministries, baptist, christ), social societies (fraternal, league, elks, legion, rotary), education (elem, educational, school, scholarship, pta, students), and charitable organizations (museum, grants, grantmaking, volunteer, nonprofit, foundations, foundation, trust).

Next we consider how this approach measures up to human coding. An ideal evaluation would be based on a careful review of each nonprofit's activities and expenditures. Given resource constraints, our approximation of this was to use crowdsourcing to evaluate whether 408 nonprofits engage in political activities. Contributors were given the name of a nonprofit (taken from the IRS manifest of nonprofit filings), asked to find the website of the organization through an Internet search, and then asked to respond to five questions.[11] We first asked if they were able to find a website unique to that organization, and then whether they found a reference to a political issue, to an elected political leader or candidate, or a political activity such as a get-out-the-vote effort.[12]

The nonprofits were chosen based on a stratified random sample to increase the proportion of political nonprofits that were evaluated. One-third of this sample were from the least likely to be political (< 0.8), one-third from the moderately political (0.8 to 0.9), and the remainder from the most likely to be political (> 0.9). The evaluation of politicality was undertaken not by the researchers directly but through crowdsourcing, using the CrowdFlower service. Among the advantages of crowdsourcing are scalability, speed, the "wisdom of the crowds" arising from multiple cod-

---

11. Internal Revenue Service, "Exempt Organizations Business Master File Extract," available at: http://www.irs.gov/Charities-&-Non-Profits/Exempt-Organizations-Business-Master-File-Extract-EO-BMF (updated March 14, 2016); and IRS, "SOI Tax Stats: Annual Extract of Tax-Exempt Organization Financial Data," available at: http://www.irs.gov/uac/SOI-Tax-Stats-Annual-Extract-of-Tax-Exempt-Organization-Financial-Data (updated May 8, 2015).

12. See the supplemental appendix (http://bit.ly/1O77GdG) for additional instructions and precise wording.

Table 1. One Hundred Most Political and Nonpolitical Words (Naive Bayes)

	Names Model	IRS Model
Nonpolitical words	charitable, foundation, organization, trust, amp, elem, box, form, _ler, school, church, scholarship, family, fbo, memorial, league, pta, private, programs, community, bank, high, club, program, ave, remainder, membership, ttee, youth, foundations, educational, middle, events, volunteer, charity, unitrust, little, ste, service, middot, rotary, nonpro_t, christian, charities, park, students, legion, areas, scholarships, mellon, society, annual, click, details, _re, ministries, arts, services, chapter, pnc, elks, clubs, location, alumni, welcome, hospital, award, housing, learning, url, library, online, located, schools, grants, avenue, order, lodge, elementary, min, music, bene_ciary, children, grade, year, baptist, grantmaking, forms, directors, application, login, recreational, history, mary, summer, gift, museum, registration, fraternal, knights	charitable, foundation, trust, organization, elem, box, form, _ler, church, bank, fbo, scholarship, amp, memorial, family, private, school, remainder, ttee, high, ave, middle, foundations, club, educational, unitrust, service, ste, areas, christian, mellon, charity, community, charities, youth, details, pnc, location, park, league, _re, nonpro_t, volunteer, mary, society, ministries, programs, program, scholarships, housing, legion, elks, avenue, religious, arts, pennsylvania, grantmaking, mall, baptist, located, membership, children, order, bene_ciary, wells, christ, nect, non, child, lodge, social, endowment, crut, students, fargo, welfare, independence, helen, tuw, recreational, clubs, lutheran, bny, ministry, fraternal, development, add, annuity, char, cemetery, little, pro_t, alumni, grants, chapter, museum, ridge, grade, elementary, grace
Political words	pac, congress, political, committee, action, house, republican, federal, party, conservative, senate, elections, democratic, congressional, super, contributions, campaign, government, committees, election, victory, candidates, america, president, inc, corporation, contributors, john, candidate, opensecrets, state, pacs, american, bill, lobbying, liberal, politics, zip, cycle, obama, states, fund, data, inuence, name, fec, money, united, americans, freedom, elect, pacnone, energy, district, presidential, new, company, executive, politicians, spending, friends, washington, individual, news, code, group, david, cash, contribution, insurance, national, summary, vote, rep, citizens, list, committeenone, brokers, richard, democrats, get, reports, leadership, york, press, top, retired, majority, analysis, total, liberty, michael, self, industry, commercial, _nance, general, sign, interest, expenditures	pac, congress, political, committee, action, house, republican, party, senate, conservative, federal, elections, democratic, congressional, super, campaign, contributions, committees, election, victory, candidates, president, government, contributors, candidate, state, america, opensecrets, bill, corporation, pacs, american, john, lobbying, liberal, news, politics, zip, states, inuence, name, cycle, obama, fec, district, money, new, americans, elect, data, health, energy, get, executive, leadership, pacnone, presidential, insurance, politicians, united, inc, spending, friends, press, individual, resources, contribution, vote, washington, cash, reports, summary, issues, code, group, rep, list, policy, committeenone, brokers, democrats, top, local, national, company, sign, retired, citizens, majority, industry, take, analysis, general, commercial, freedom, blog, primary, _nance, law, self

Source: Authors' calculations.

ers, and the inability of researchers to bias the results in their favor.

On the other hand, especially if not well supervised, crowdsourcing can suffer from a lack of sophistication or attention by contributors.[13] Many different algorithms have been proposed for aggregating the results of crowdsourced data. Kenneth Benoit and his colleagues (forthcoming) provide a review of such methods and suggest that for their purposes a simple averaging approach is roughly comparable to more complex methods. Given that the CrowdFlower screens responses based on an adaptive algorithm, our approach is simply to use majority vote among the evaluators who passed the screening process and evaluated the data. Thus, we label a nonprofit as political if a majority of the CrowdFlower contributors identified any of the three indicators—mentions of political issues, political leaders or candidates, or political activities.

Of the fifty-five people who attempted to contribute to the project, eighteen did not pass the initial screening, which is aimed at removing contributors who simply guess randomly. Those who did pass provided 1,442 trusted judgments. Each organization was reviewed by at least three different individuals. Contributors seem to have been reasonably satisfied with the clarity of the instructions, the pay, and the quality of the test questions: the nineteen contributors who chose to evaluate our study rated it as 4 out of 5 on average. For the following analysis, we generally label as political those nonprofits that receive a rating of 0.99 or higher on our index, but we present results across other possible cutoffs on the theory that the success of one's intended use depends on a willingness to trade off Type I and Type II error.

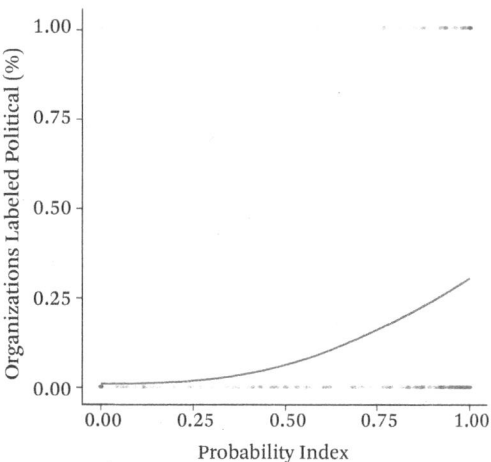

Figure 1. Nonprofit Organizations Labeled Political Based on CrowdFlower Majority Vote

Source: Authors' calculations.

We begin with a very simple sanity check: are there more political nonprofits at higher levels of our index? Figure 1 shows that this is indeed the case: the proportion of political organizations increases from 10 to more than 40 percent as our measure increases. This suggests that some political nonprofits are not correctly labeled as such by our measure. We examine this possibility by looking at the operating characteristics of our measure. To provide a baseline we compare our scores against the (name/keyword) labels we used in training, based on self-reporting to the IRS and keyword searches using the organizations' names, as described earlier.

A good measure not only is good at identifying political groups (that is, it has few false negatives) but also does not falsely report a nonpolitical group as political (it has a low false positive rate). With this in mind, in figure

---

13. To address this we required that respondents be in the United States, be of the highest competence among CrowdFlower contributors ("highest quality"), and be removed from the set of contributors if they answered questions too quickly. Contributors were also required to maintain at least 66 percent accuracy while participating, as well as to answer six questions as a pretest before their answers were counted as part of the data set. Even after passing this initial screening, contributors could still be judged to be "untrustworthy" based on an algorithm proprietary to CrowdFlower that makes any use of test questions for which the correct answer is known ex ante. These test questions were based on organizations that were clearly either political or nonpolitical, such as the American Energy Alliance (which describes itself as an "organization that engages in grassroots public policy advocacy and debate concerning energy and environmental policies") and Grand Ledge Area Youth Football Inc. (a small nonpolitical organization that supports a sports league).

Figure 2. Validation by Independent Evaluation of Whether 366 Nonprofit Organizations Are Political or Nonpolitical

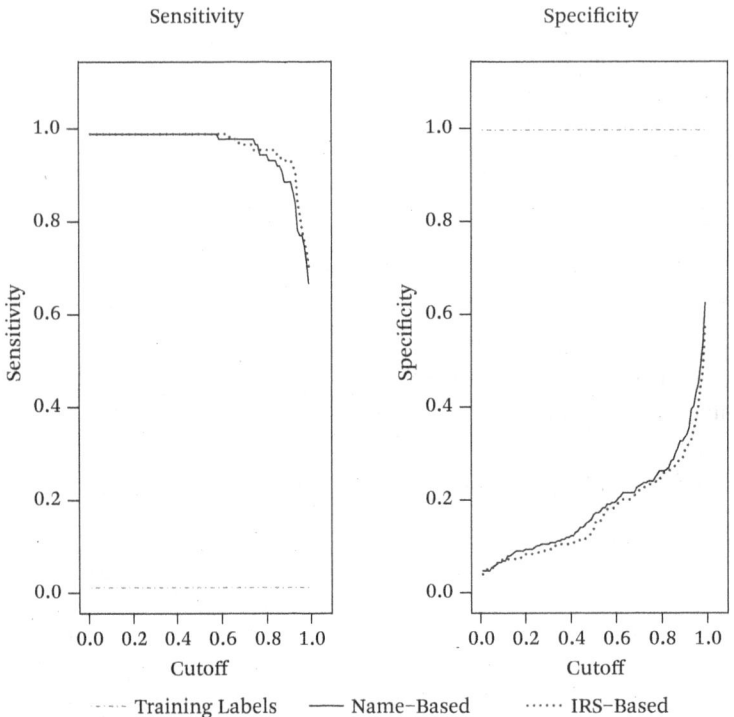

Source: Authors' calculations.

2 we present two measures of evaluation for the training labels and our two measures (trained using the labels from name keywords and from self-disclosure to the IRS) and consider how well the measures perform across different cutoff levels for our politicality index. Evaluations of sensitivity (the number of true positives divided by true positives and false negatives), on the left, suggest that our measure does considerably better than our training labels in picking up organizations that are indeed political. That is, conditional on an organization being political, our algorithm does a substantially better job of predicting this politicality.

Evaluations of specificity (the number of true negatives divided by true negatives and false positives) appear on the right side of the figure. This result implies that, conditional on being nonpolitical, our algorithm is able to retain most of the power in detecting nonpolitical organizations. Given that fewer than 25 percent of all nonprofit organizations are political, guessing that no organizations are political can ensure a high specificity; this is why the initial training labels (which label only half a percent of organizations as political) do well, as seen on the top right. The IRS- and name-based methods are fairly similar on all measures, though the model based on name-based training labels performs slightly better. This similarity is due to the large number of PACs included in the training data as examples of political organizations.

The key takeaway is that, even with a high threshold, we are able to greatly improve on recall without overly sacrificing on specificity. That is, we can identify a lot of political organizations with few false positives. In using common machine learning metrics to balance sensitivity and specificity, we ultimately chose a threshold of 0.99. For the IRS-based model, we correctly classify 85 percent of political organizations, whereas our training labels based on self-disclosure to the IRS identify only 8 percent. We incorrectly classify more groups as political than the training labels do, but only because the IRS rarely labels any group as political. Given the challenges of this classification task, false positives are unavoidable. Our model still correctly identifies nonpolitical groups 57 percent of the time. The IRS labels have very high specificity (about 98 percent), but note that guessing that all nonprofits are nonpolitical will ensure that 100 percent of nonpolitical nonprofits are identified as such, yet the measure will have no utility.

Finally, we note that while the CrowdFlower approach is useful for validating our measure on a small data set, it is not feasible as a replacement for our method. The cost of obtaining three ratings for each organization in the validation set (including some by coders deemed untrustworthy and subsequently discarded) averaged $0.43 per organization. Assuming fixed marginal costs, scaling this to the 339,818 organizations we analyze would cost about $146,121.

HOW MUCH IS SPENT AND BY WHOM?

For the first aggregate look at the politicality of nonprofits, we examine the politicality of strata determined by the subsection of the U.S. code under which organizations are organized and program areas are operationalized through the National Taxonomy of Exempt Entities (NTEE) codes. Examples of these codes are "Educational Institutions," "Crime, Legal Related," "Animal Related," and so forth. There are twenty-six distinct broad classification codes, and each one is associated with a number of subcodes that identify more specifically the type of work a nonprofit does. This taxonomy is self-reported. Approximately one-third of the organizations in our study are not given NTEE codes in the data released by the IRS, and so they are excluded from any subsequent analysis that requires these codings.

Figure 3 provides a sense of the program areas and subsections that most often tend to be political. Each axis is ordered such that, marginalizing over the other axis, the categories become increasingly political as they get farther from the origin in the lower left. Thus, veterans' organizations and labor unions are the subsections with the highest proportion of political organizations. Likewise, social science research institutes and civil rights, social action, and advocacy organizations have the highest rates of politicality among NTEE classes. Unshaded strata indicate an insufficient sample size (fewer than 50 groups) to demonstrate meaningful patterns in the data.

It is informative to specifically examine the distribution of political groups organized under subsection 4: social welfare organizations. Crucially, organizations dealing with the environment that are organized under this subsection are very likely to be political in nature, as are organizations classified as civil rights, social action, or advocacy groups. This is unsurprising. A conservation group that works to, for instance, maintain parks or trails will find it beneficial to organize under subsection 3 to gain tax advantages for donors (who can deduct contributions from their own taxes). However, such benefits come with increased scrutiny and decreased freedom to take overt political action (such as donating to political candidates' PACs). It is natural, then, for groups concerned with environmental policy to organize under subsection 4, which allows for broad flexibility to exert political action. The increased politicality of environmental 501(c)(4)s relative to 501(c)(3)s bears out this story. This provides some initial evidence of organizational movement between subsections based on the scope of a nonprofit's activities.

To get a sense of the geographic distribution of political nonprofits, we examine the states in which organizations are headquartered. This is, of course, a rough measure, given that national organizations are likely to be headquartered in New York City or Washington, D.C., yet are also likely to be interested in policy outcomes throughout the country. We examine this geographical distribution in figure 4. In general, more organizations exist where there are more people, and the figure thus resembles a population map of the United States.

To look at this in a more fine-grained way, figure 5 shows the number of groups in a given state for every 100,000 individuals in that state. A number of features stand out. First, very low-population states in the Great Plains, such as Montana and Wyoming, appear to have a rela-

Figure 3. Proportion of Political Nonprofit Organizations by Type

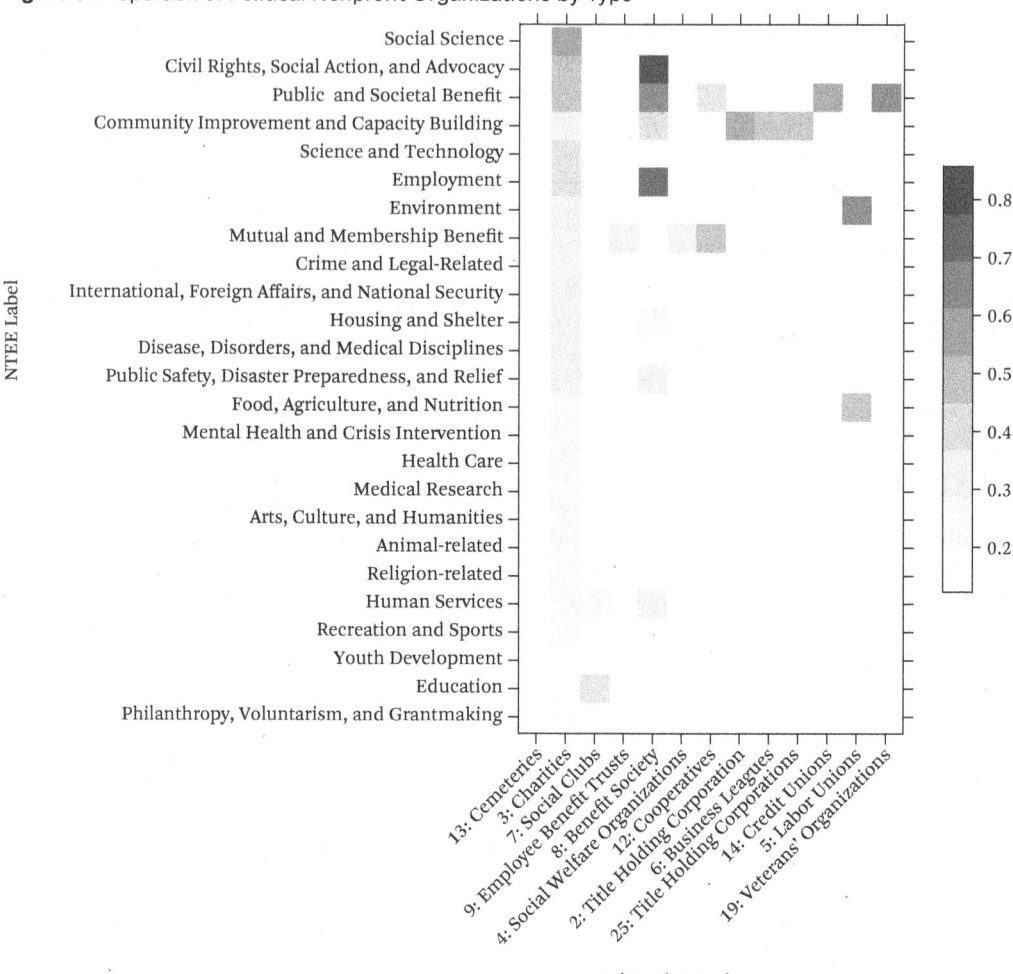

Source: Authors' calculations.

tively high number of political organizations given their size. The Northeast dominates the map with more organizations per capita than most of the rest of the country. Unsurprisingly, Washington, D.C., also has a large number of organizations relative to its population, possibly as a result of nationally oriented nonprofits being centered in the Northeast combined with a base level of nonprofit political activity in every state. That is, certain organizations (such as veterans' organizations, Elk lodges, and some advocacy groups) tend to have at least one local chapter in each state but add additional registered nonprofits in response to state characteristics other than its population.

We use our measure to create an estimate of the political money spent by nonprofits, or politically adjusted revenue. This estimate relies on three key elements. We begin with revenue data provided for each nonprofit by the IRS. We then use our index of the likelihood of each organization being involved in politics, as validated by the crowdsourced evaluations.[14] Finally, we need an estimate of the percentage

---

14. That is, for a given nonprofit, PAR is the product of revenue, an indicator for whether the group is political (greater than 0.99 on our politicality score), 0.4215 (the precision of our score), and the fraction of the average political group's budget that is actually devoted to political aims. This is not a way to estimate individual nonprofits precisely, but we believe that it provides a rough estimate for the aggregate spending of organizations.

Figure 4. Number of Political Nonprofit Organizations by State

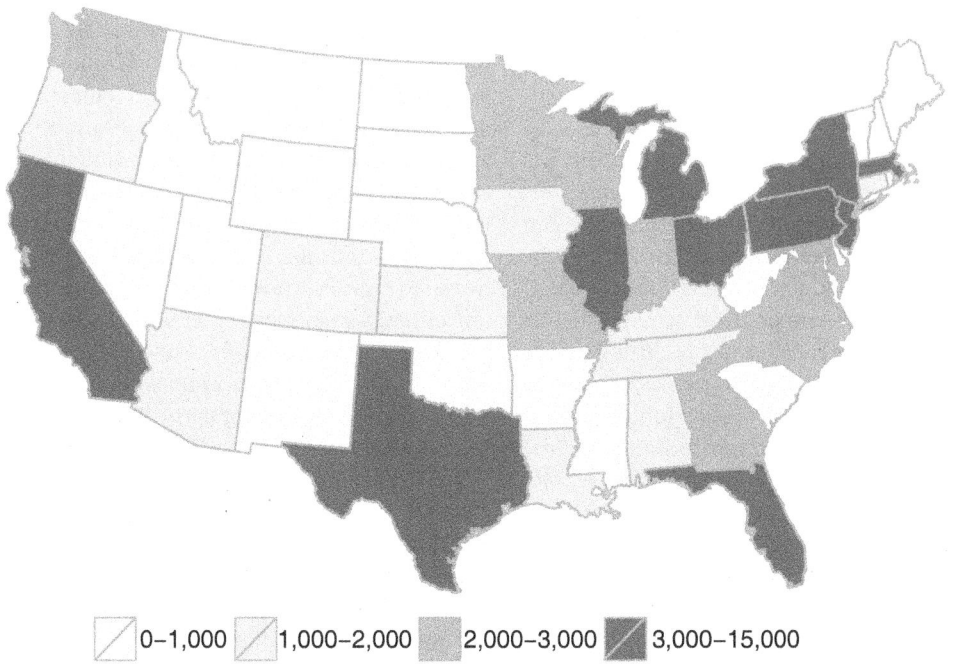

0–1,000   1,000–2,000   2,000–3,000   3,000–15,000

Source: Authors' calculations.

Figure 5. Number of Political Nonprofit Organizations per 100,000 Population

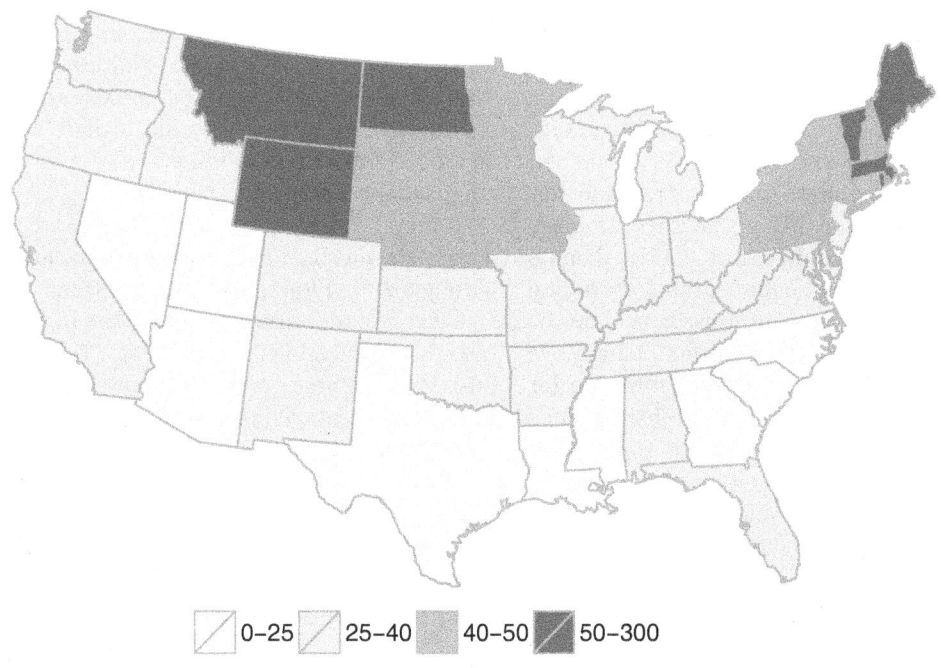

0–25   25–40   40–50   50–300

Source: Authors' calculations.

of each nonprofit's budget that goes toward political activity. We have no particular data from which to make this estimate, nor is there any clear way to do it, so we simply use a figure of 1 percent and invite readers to adjust our estimates according to their prior beliefs. For example, those who believe that nonprofits spend 0.1 percent (or one-tenth-of-one percent) of their budget on political activities can divide the numbers in figure 6 or figure 7 by 10. We expect that some organizations spend less than 1 percent on political activities, while others spend more. For example, 501(c)(3) nonprofits are allowed to spend between 5 and 20 percent of their expenditures on lobbying without jeopardizing their nonprofit status.[15] While not representative of nonprofits as a whole, Crossroads GPS spent nearly half of its budget on direct political expenditure and much of the remainder on grants to other political organizations. Given that organizations' budgets are included in our estimate of PAR conditional on being classified as political through our algorithm, we interpret PAR as a conservative estimate of the actual political expenditure of nonprofits.

Furthermore, we assume that three types of organizations spend none of their budgets on politics. We exclude all NTEE-coded health or general rehabilitation organizations (like hospitals), educational institutions (like university endowments), and human services organizations (like the Red Cross). These organizations probably spend some amount of money on politics, but the sheer amount of revenue they generate makes it likely that they devote a much smaller fraction of it to politics than do other organizations in our sample. Including these groups increases our estimates, but by less than an order of magnitude. Finally, we must also assume that any organization for which we were unable to find a website spends no money on politics. This assumption is quite plausible considering that these organizations tend to be either very small or organized as a very closely held trust (and are thus unlikely to be politically engaged).

Figure 6 shows the breakdown of money across strata defined by program area (operationalized by NTEE code) and the subsection of the tax code under which groups are organized. It is important to note that some strata are relatively sparse and that PAR is most reliable when larger numbers of organizations are aggregated. Compounding this difficulty is that NTEE codes are missing for a large fraction of our sample. Nonetheless, a number of patterns stand out. First, 501(c)(3) organizations consistently have the largest PAR. This is not entirely surprising considering the large number and diversity of these organizations. They tend to have larger budgets than groups organized under different parts of the tax code. Among these groups, the two program areas which are associated with the highest PAR are 'Science and Technology Research Institutes' and 'International Foreign Affairs and National Security'. The latter clearly encompasses a political/policy dimension and is unsurprising. The former consists of many industry and professional associations. One example of an organization of this type imputed to be political is the American Society of Mechanical Engineers (ASME), a 501(c)(3) professional organization for mechanical engineers. We impute a PAR for ASME of $400k in 2011, which may seem high prima facie. In that same year, however, ASME disclosed $214k in lobbying expenditures (Center for Responsive Politics 2011). This suggests our estimate is unlikely to be overly high, given that it would include any state-level lobbying and issue advocacy campaigns that ASME may engage in.

It may be surprising that program areas with high rates of politicality are associated with (generally) lower PAR, but not when we consider that they receive relatively less money than do organizations of other types. To demonstrate that these groups still represent significant political spending, we break down the civil rights, social action, and advocacy label (a program type with high rates of politicality) to its constituent subcodes in figure 7 to identify more specifically the issue areas on which these groups focus. The figure demonstrates the distribution of money among organiza-

---

15. Internal Revenue Service, "Measuring Lobbying Activity: Expenditure Test," available at: http://www.irs.gov/Charities-&-Non-Profits/Measuring-Lobbying-Activity:-Expenditure-Test (last updated March 28, 2016).

Figure 6. Politically Adjusted Revenue of Nonprofit Organizations by Type

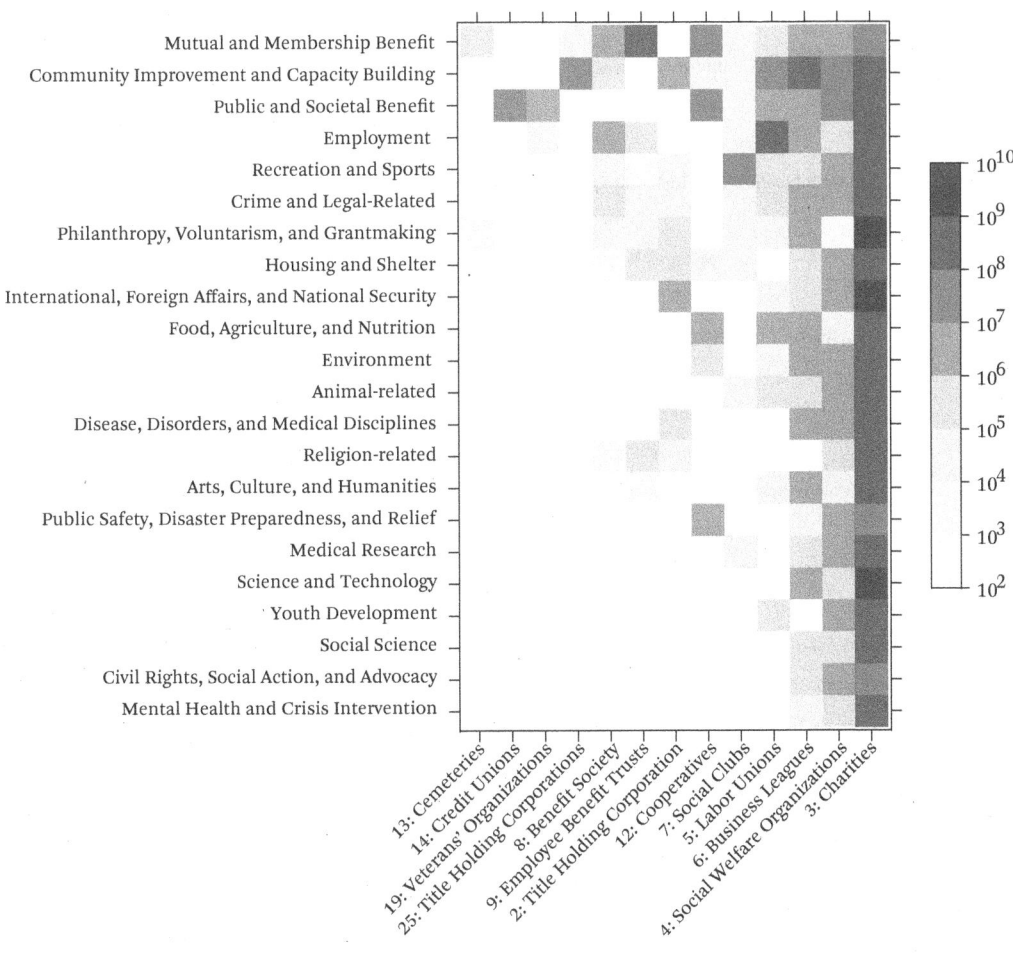

Source: Authors' calculations.

tions with this NTEE label by issue area. It should be noted that PAR is likely to underrepresent the amount of money these groups devote to politics if they devote more than 1 percent of their budget to politics. Civil liberties advocacy groups are estimated to have a much higher PAR than other groups with this NTEE label, which subsumes groups like the American Civil Liberties Union as well as Second Amendment advocacy groups. Since organizations may choose where to place themselves, these categories are not as cleanly discriminating as might be hoped. For instance, many organizations choose to place themselves in the more general civil rights category than a more specific category that might also apply to them. Nevertheless, figure 7 gives some perspective on the relative PAR across issue areas.

Aggregating over all strata provides an estimate of the total PAR by nonprofits of $760 million in 2011. This number may be compared to the Center for Responsive Politics' estimate of the direct political expenditure of nonprofit organizations of $309 million for the entire 2012 election cycle (that is, 2011 and 2012). It may also be compared to the total amount raised by PACs in the 2012 cycle of $1.4 billion, or the amount raised by candidates' PACs of $453.3 million (Center for Responsive Politics, n.d.). Although this estimate is not precise, the amount of dark money being spent during modern election cycles is clearly large enough

Figure 7. Politically Adjusted Revenue for Nonprofit Civil Rights, Social Action, and Advocacy Organizations

Source: Authors' calculations.

that it must be accounted for to properly assess the role of money in the American political system. It is a striking finding that our conservative estimate of the political activity of nonprofits is in fact higher than extant estimates. That fact can be squared with the CPR's estimates by understanding the loose regulatory framework in which nonprofits operate. The vast majority of this spending need not be reported.

CONCLUSION

The mechanics of political spending in congressional and presidential races is rapidly changing as laws and court rulings have made possible new approaches and organizational forms. Understanding how such activity redraws the political map requires being able to identify the relevant actors involved and the resources they expend even as such organizations aim to avoid public transparency. Existing approaches based on the names of organizations or self-reported activity vastly underestimate the degree to which organizations involve themselves in politics. We have developed a novel approach to classifying the political status of nonprofits based not merely on their voluntary self-disclosure but also on the text of their websites. This measure provides vital leverage in understanding the scope of this increasingly controversial type of political engagement. In seeking to validate this measure by allowing independent coders to determine whether a random sample of nonprofits are political, we find that, even though our measure is imperfect, it does a significantly better job of determining nonprofits' political status than using disclosures to the IRS or searches based on nonprofit names.

With these estimates in hand, we provide an overview of the nonprofits involved in political activity by issue area and geography. The relatively recent nature of the changes we describe makes it difficult to know whether the patterns we identify in the last few years will continue. Nevertheless, the political spending of nonprofits is substantial and growing, and we must grapple with it in order to understand interest group politics today.[16] Future work ought to identify variation in the type and extent of political engagement among those nonprofits we identify, as well as the relationship of these organizations to other political actors and the strategies of political campaigns.

REFERENCES

Ansolabehere, Steven, et al. 2004. "Did Firms Profit from Soft Money?" *Election Law Journal* 3(2): 193–98.

Benoit, Kenneth, Drew Conway, Benjamin E. Lauderdale, Michael Laver, and Slava Mikhaylov. Forthcoming. "Crowd-Sourced Text Analysis: Reproducible and Agile Production of Political Data." *American Political Science Review*.

Center for Responsive Politics. 2011. "American Society of Mechanical Engineers: Client Summary: 2011." Available at: http://www.opensecrets.org/lobby/clientsum.php?id=D000047049&year=2011 (data updated April 20, 2015).

Center for Responsive Politics. N.d. "Political Action Committees." Available at: https://www.opensecrets.org/pacs/ (accessed July 25, 2016).

Dimmery, Drew, and Andrew Peterson. 2014. "Spending Swept Under the Rug: Inferring Political Ideology of Ostensibly Non-partisan Organizations." Poster presentation at the thirty-first annual summer methods meeting of the Society for Political Methodology. University of Georgia, Athens. (July 23–26).

Drawbaugh, Kevin, and Kim Dixon. 2014. "IRS Kept Shifting Targets in Tax-Exempt Groups Scrutiny: Report." *Reuters*, May 13.

Edsall, Thomas B. 2014. "Who Needs a Smoke-Filled Room? Karl Rove, the Koch Brothers, and the End of Transparency." *New York Times*, September 9.

Gold, Matea. 2013. "FEC Deadlocks, for Now, on Whether Political Committees Can Accept Bitcoin." *Washington Post*, November 21.

Greenacre, Michael J. 1984. *Theory and Applications of Correspondence Analysis*. London: Academic Press.

Grimmer, Justin, and Brandon M. Stewart. 2013. "Text as Data: The Promise and Pitfalls of Automatic Content Analysis Methods for Political Texts." *Political Analysis* 21(3): 267–97.

Hastie, Trevor, Robert Tibshirani, and Jerome Friedman. 2009. *The Elements of Statistical Learning: Data Mining, Inference, and Prediction*, 2nd ed. New York: Springer.

Kollman, Ken. 1998. *Outside Lobbying: Public Opinion and Interest Group Strategies*. Princeton, N.J.: Princeton University Press.

LaPira, Timothy, and Herschel Thomas III. 2014. "Revolving Door Lobbyists and Interest Representation." *Interest Groups and Advocacy* 3(1): 4–29.

Lipton, Eric, et al. 2014. "Foreign Powers Buy Influence at Think Tanks." *New York Times*, September 7.

Lowe, Will. 2008. "Understanding Wordscores." *Political Analysis* 16(4): 356–71.

Magleby, David B., and J. Qin Monson, eds. 2004. *The Last Hurrah? Soft Money and Issue Advocacy in the 2002 Congressional Elections*. Washington, D.C.: Brookings Institution Press.

Maguire, Robert. 2014a. "Dark Money Hits $50 Million, Most Still to Come," Center for Responsive Politics, August 28. Available at: https://www.opensecrets.org/news/2014/08/dark-money-hits-50-million-most-still-to-come (accessed September 1, 2014).

———. 2014b. "Outside Groups, Dark Money Organizations Fuel 2014 Midterms." Center for Responsive Politics, September 4. Available at: https://www.opensecrets.org/news/2014/09/outside-groups-dark-money-organizations-fuel-2014-midterms (accessed September 9, 2014).

Pedregosa, Fabian, et al. 2011. "Scikit-learn: Machine Learning in Python." *Journal of Machine Learning Research* 12 (October): 2825–30.

Planned Parenthood Federation of America, Inc. 2012. "IRS Form 990: Return of Organization Exempt from Income Tax." Available at: http://www.plannedparenthood.org/files/2413/9620/1318/PPFA_FY13_Final_990_public_disclosure.pdf (accessed August 9, 2016).

Ramey, Adam Joseph, and Lawrence S. Rothenberg. N.d. "The Tangled Web of Policy Support: Foundations and Environmental NGOs." Working paper. New York University at Abu Dhabi and University of Rochester. Available at: http://www

---

16. For one direction of future work, see Dimmery and Peterson (2014).

.adamramey.com/uploads/1/3/6/4/1364451/tangled_web_v2_4.pdf (accessed July 25, 2016).

Rennie, Jason D. M., Lawrence Shih, Jaime Teevan, and David R. Karger. 2003. "Tackling the Poor Assumptions of Naive Bayes Text Classifiers." In *Proceedings of the Twentieth International Conference on Machine Learning,* edited by Tom Fawcett and Nina Mishra. Menlo Park, Calif.: AAAI Press.

Salant, Jonathan D. 2009. "FEC Deadlock May Increase Clout of Independent Political Groups." *Bloomberg News,* May 23.

Stratmann, Thomas. 2010. "Do Low Contribution Limits Insulate Incumbents from Competition?" *Election Law Journal* 9(2): 125–40.

Zhang, Huajie. 2004. "The Optimality of Naive Bayes." In *Proceedings of the Seventeenth International Florida Artificial Intelligence Research Society Conference,* edited by Valerie Barr and Zdravko Marko. Menlo Park, Calif.: AAAI Press.

Home Truths: Promises and Challenges in Linking Mortgages and Political Influence

DENIZ IGAN

What can "big data" tell us about the dynamics shaping the regulation of and activities in housing and mortgage markets? This paper describes a detailed database of the lobbying activities, campaign contributions, political connections, and mortgage lending activities of the financial industry. A review of the findings of recent research that has utilized this data set suggests that the political influence of the financial industry may have a bearing on the regulation of mortgage markets and, in turn, on risk-taking by lenders. A key challenge is deciphering the motivations behind the politically targeted activities of the financial industry.

Keywords: lobbying, political influence, mortgage lending, financial regulation

It is impossible to think about regulation and policy frameworks without thinking about the political economy factors that shape them. The public-interest theory of regulation depicts government intervention as a correction to market inefficiencies to maximize social welfare. But regulation is not written in a vacuum and may be influenced by private-interest groups, so much so that rent extraction at the expense of others actually ends up reducing social welfare.

Finance offers a particularly interesting opportunity to study the political economy of regulation. Financial regulation is well justified by the market failures stemming from moral hazard, asymmetric information, and systemic risk. Indeed, costly financial crises—often alleged to be a consequence of inadequate regulation and ineffective supervision—attest to the importance of well-functioning, resilient financial markets. The financial industry's interference in the design and implementation of specific regulations may be related to financial crises because special-interest groups may tailor the financial regulatory landscape to better fit their own needs and may also take excessive risks under lax regulations that they helped to enact (Acemoglu 2009; Calomiris 2009; Johnson 2009).

Establishing a link between political influence and financial regulation and risk-taking in a formal setup, especially with the backdrop of the recent financial crisis, is an intriguing exercise, but it is often constrained by the lack of readily available, detailed information on politically targeted activities. That task has been taken up, however, in a recent strand of literature by researchers who have meticulously invested in merging different data sets to connect the dots.

This paper describes a detailed database of a rather comprehensive data set documenting the political influence of the finance, insurance, and real estate (FIRE) industry in the

Deniz Igan is deputy division chief at the International Monetary Fund.

I am grateful to Atif Mian, Prachi Mishra, Howard Rosenthal, and participants in the Russell Sage Foundation "Big Data in Political Economy" conference for useful comments and suggestions. The views expressed here are my own and do not represent those of the IMF or IMF policy. Direct correspondence to: Deniz Igan at digan @imf.org, 700 19th St. NW, Washington, D.C., 20431.

United States, legislative actions related to financial regulation, and mortgage lending activities by politically active financial institutions from 1999 through 2006.

The paper then gives an account of recent research utilizing this data set. There are many interesting questions one can ask regarding not only the process shaping the regulatory framework but also the outcomes realized against the backdrop of the resultant regulatory framework. For instance, are politically targeted activities by FIRE institutions linked to the legislative outcomes of bills on financial regulation? Do legislators' network connections with the financial industry and its lobbyists affect their decisions to support or oppose certain proposals? Is the risk-taking behavior of lenders that lobby different from that of lenders not engaged in lobbying? How did these lobbying lenders perform in 2008 when turmoil hit financial markets? Do lobbying and other politically targeted activities by FIRE institutions make information-sharing possible, thus facilitating "better" financial regulation and fostering mortgage market development?

The studies summarized here answer some but not all of these questions. The findings so far suggest that the political influence of the financial industry has a bearing on the regulation of mortgage markets and, in turn, on lenders' risk-taking. In particular, the legislative proposals that were in favor of deregulation and on which more lobbying dollars were spent were more likely to be signed into law. In this more relaxed regulatory environment, lenders that lobbied took larger risks and suffered worse losses. This may seem to support the popular interpretation that regulatory capture paves the way to costly financial crises.

A key challenge, however, is deciphering the motivations behind the politically targeted activities of the financial industry. Doing so could shed some light on the question of whether these activities improve social welfare. The paper concludes with a discussion of possible directions that future research could take.

CONSTRUCTING A DATA SET OF POLITICAL INFLUENCE, FINANCIAL REGULATION, AND MORTGAGE LENDING

Many of the data sources commonly used to analyze the political economy of financial regulation and mortgage markets have been around for years. What arguably has changed is the increased computational capacity that facilitates the merging of different data sets and allows more sophisticated analyses of existing data sets.[1]

In what follows, I describe in detail the main data sets for analyzing the political influence of financial institutions, legislative actions on financial regulation, and mortgage lending. I then explain how these data sets have been merged in order to study particular linkages.

Political Influence

An individual, firm, or other entity can influence the political and legislative process in various ways. Here I focus on three activities: campaign contributions, lobbying, and networking.

Campaign Contributions

In the United States, special-interest groups and other private entities, including individuals, can make campaign finance contributions, in particular through political action committees (PACs). PACs, often representing special-interest groups, are organized for the purpose of raising and spending money to elect—or sometimes defeat—particular candidates. The total amount that PACs can contribute to an individual candidate's committee is capped: it cannot exceed $5,000 per election (primary, general, or special). Similarly, a PAC cannot give more than $15,000 annually to any national party committee or more than $5,000 annually to any other PAC. On the receiving side, a PAC may receive up to $5,000 from any one individual, PAC, or party committee per calendar year. These limits are applied on a consolidated basis to affiliated PACs by treating them all as one entity.

Data on PAC contributions are available

---

1. Space limitations prohibit a thorough review of the literature that has utilized some of the data sets used here. For two recent papers that are worth mentioning for their innovative methods in exploiting the data, see Bonica (2016) on campaign contributions and Agarwal et al. (2012) on the Home Mortgage Disclosure Act (HMDA).

through the Federal Election Commission (FEC) and the Center for Responsive Politics (CRP). PACs can be linked to a corporate or industry sponsor as well as, naturally, to a legislator. Compiling the data from these sources is relatively straightforward, and such data have been utilized to a considerable extent in the political economy literature.[2]

Lobbying Expenditures
In addition to campaign contributions, individuals, companies, and special-interest groups can legally influence the policy formation process by carrying out lobbying activities in the executive and legislative branches of the federal government. Some special interests hire lobbying firms; others have lobbyists working in-house. These lobbying activities, albeit accounting for the bulk of politically targeted expenditures, have received less attention in the literature.

With the passage of the Lobbying Disclosure Act (LDA) of 1995, individual companies and organizations have been required to provide a substantial amount of information on their lobbying activities. Since 1996, all lobbyists (intermediaries who lobby on behalf of companies and organizations) have had to file semiannual reports to the Senate Office of Public Records (SOPR), listing the name of each of their clients (firms), the total income they have received from each client, and the specific issues that are the focus of their lobbying efforts. In parallel, all firms with in-house lobbying departments are required to file similar reports stating the total dollar amount they have spent (either in-house or in payments to external lobbyists). LDA requires the disclosure of not only the dollar amounts actually received and spent but also the issues targeted by lobbying activity. Thus, unlike PAC contributions, the lobbying expenditures of companies can be associated with very specific, targeted policy areas.

The data are based on the semiannual lobbying disclosure reports filed with the SOPR and can be compiled from two sources: the SOPR website and the website of the Center for Responsive Politics. The CRP website provides information on lobbying expenditures as well as on the general issues with which lobbying is associated. However, the information is not user-friendly (for example, getting details requires clicking on each firm name) and often has to be cross-checked with individual lobbying reports, which are publicly available in PDF format on the SOPR website. Moreover, the CRP does not provide information on the specific issues (or particular regulations) with which the lobbying is associated. Hence, one first needs to extract the entire lobbying database from the CRP website—comprising about 16,000 unique firms over the period 1999–2006, with a maximum of around 9,000 firms in any one year—and then determine those firms for which more detailed information is needed to address the research question at hand. For instance, after matching firms with mortgage lending activities in the HMDA database, one would then examine the individual PDF reports of the approximately 250 matched firms to extract detailed information, including specific issues.[3]

LDA requires lobbying firms and organizations to register and file reports of their lobbying activities not only with the Secretary of the Senate (in the SOPR) but also the Clerk of the House of Representatives. In general, it requires registration by an individual lobbyist (or the lobbyist's employer if the firm employs one or more lobbyists) within forty-five days after the lobbyist first makes—or is employed or retained to make—a lobbying contact with the president, the vice president, a member of Congress, or any other specified federal officer or employee, including certain high-ranking members of the uniformed services.

A registrant must file a report for the semiannual period in which registration initially occurred and for each semiannual period thereafter, including the period during which registration terminates. Lobbying firms—entities with one or more lobbyists, including self-

---

2. Note that focusing only on PACs probably understates politically targeted activities through campaign contributions because individual contributions (for example, from principals at closely held mortgage lenders) are not included.

3. It would be possible to at least partially automate this process using Python or similar software.

employed individuals who act as lobbyists for outside clients—are required to file a separate report for each client covered by a registration. Organizations employing in-house lobbyists file a single report for each semiannual period. The semiannual report must be filed no later than forty-five days after the end of the semiannual period beginning on the first day of January and the first day of July of every year in which a registrant is registered. LDA requires the Secretary of the Senate and the Clerk of the House of Representatives to make all registrations and reports available to the public as soon as practicable after they are received.

Under section 3(10) of the LDA, an individual is defined as a "lobbyist" with respect to a particular client if he or she makes more than one lobbying contact (more than one communication to a covered official) and the individual's "lobbying activities" constitute at least 20 percent of his or her time in services for that client over any six-month period. "Lobbying activity" is defined in section 3(7) of the LDA as "lobbying contacts or efforts in support of such contacts, including background work that is intended, at the time it was performed, for use in contacts, and coordination with the lobbying activities of others."

Lobbying firms are required to provide a good-faith estimate rounded to the nearest $20,000 of all lobbying-related income in each six-month period. Likewise, organizations that hire lobbyists must provide a good-faith estimate rounded to the nearest $20,000 of all lobbying-related expenditures in a six-month period. An organization or a lobbying firm that spends less than $10,000 in any six-month period does not have to state its expenditures. In those cases, CRP treats the figure as zero.

The CRP calculates annual lobbying expenditures and incomes (of lobbying firms) by adding midyear totals and year-end totals. Whenever a lobbying report is amended, the CRP generally uses income and expense figures from the amendment instead of those from the original filing. Often, however, CRP staff determine that the income and expenditures on the amendment or termination report are inaccurate. In those instances, the CRP uses figures from the original filing.

Occasionally, income that an outside lobbying firm reports receiving from a client is greater than the client's reported lobbying expenditures. Many such discrepancies can be attributed to filer error. In cases not already resolved in previous reports, and where the discrepancy exceeds the $20,000 that can be attributed to rounding, the CRP uses the client's expenditure total rather than the lobbying firm's reported income. The only exception is when a client reports no lobbying expenditures, while the outside lobbying firm lists an actual payment. In such cases, the CRP uses the figure reported by the lobbying firm.

When the data appear to contain errors, the CRP consults official Senate records and, when necessary, contacts the SOPR or the lobbying organizations for clarification. The CRP standardizes variations in names of individuals and organizations to clearly identify them and more accurately represent their total lobbying expenditures.

Where both a parent and its subsidiary organizations lobby or hire lobbyists, the CRP attributes lobbying spending to the parent organization. Therefore, the lobbying totals reported by the CRP for a parent organization may not reflect its original filing with the Senate, but rather the combined expenditures of all related entities. However, to calculate lobbying expenditures by sector and industry, the CRP counts each subsidiary within its own sector and industry, not those of its parent. The CRP makes this distinction when it has the information necessary to distinguish some or all of the subsidiary's lobbying expenditures from either the subsidiary's own filing or the receipts reported by outside lobbying firms. For example, before tobacco giant Altria Group spun off Kraft Foods in 2007, Altria's original filing included lobbying for Kraft in its expenditures, but in the data set the CRP isolated Kraft's payments to outside lobbyists and included them under "Food Processing and Sales."

Researchers using the CRP data often face two questions: first, how to treat mergers during election cycles, and, second, how to treat trade associations. The standard procedures used are as follows. When companies merge within any two-year election cycle, their lobbying expenditures are combined and attributed to the new entity in order to correlate lobbying data with campaign contribution data for each particular organization and industry.

In addition to firms' lobbying expenditures, lobbying expenditures by FIRE trade associations—such as the Electronic Check Clearing House Organization (ECCHO) and the Financial Services Roundtable—are of interest. To split the total association expenditures among the various association members, first membership information from approximately 150 association websites are obtained. For example, according to its website, ECCHO has more than 2,200 members, including Bank of America, Citibank, and SunTrust. Next, a share of the associations' lobbying expenditures is assigned to each of their member firms by dividing each firm's lobbying expenditures by the sum of all association members' lobbying expenditures. Then, for each firm and each year, the firm's share is multiplied by its association's total lobbying expenditures so that the association lobbying expenditures are distributed across all of the member firms.[4]

Interestingly, the LDA also requires an organization to state the issues on which the registrant engaged in lobbying during the reporting period. At least one issue must be entered by the registrant or filer from the LDA's list of seventy-six issues. When a filer lists more than one issue, a separate page of the form for each code selected must be submitted.

Under each general issue heading, the filer must also list the specific issues for which lobbying activity occurred during the semiannual period—for example, by listing specific bills before Congress or specific executive branch actions.

Legislative Actions on Financial Regulation

Research on the political economy of financial regulation focuses on five general lobbying issues: accounting, banking, bankruptcy, housing, and financial institutions. Moreover, certain House and Senate bills are of particular interest since they promote either tight or lax restrictions in these five general areas of interest.

Bills that introduce tight restrictions on lenders focus primarily on predatory lending practices and high-cost mortgages. For example, many bills contain restrictions or limits on annual percentage rates for mortgages, negative amortization, prepayment penalties, balloon payments, late fees, or the financing of mortgage points and fees. Some of these bills introduce expanded consumer disclosure requirements regarding high-cost mortgages (such as including the total cost of lender fees on loan settlement paperwork or disclosing to consumers that they are borrowing at a higher interest rate).

Many of the bills prohibit high-cost mortgage lenders from engaging in other unfair or deceptive practices. Creditors are to evaluate each consumer's ability to repay a loan before making the loan, and one bill stipulates that mortgage debt is not to exceed 50 percent of an individual's income and income is to be verified. Creditors are not to encourage consumers to default on loans; moreover, mortgage lenders and other creditors must report their consumers' payment histories to credit reporting agencies. High-cost mortgage lenders may not accelerate a consumer's debt if the consumer is making payments on time. In addition, individuals who provide mortgage lending or brokerage services must be adequately trained in high-cost lending. Civil penalties for engaging in predatory lending practices are increased.

Some of the bills that firms and associations have lobbied for are closely related, as it is common for various versions of the same bill to come in front of the House or Senate in the legislative process. To exploit any information that might be contained in these different discussions of a specific issue, groups of bills that have the same name (or very similar names) or contain essentially the same language are identified. For example, the following bills are considered to be in the same group: the Predatory Lending Consumer Protection Act of 2000 (S. 2415), the Predatory Lending Consumer Protection Act of 2000 (H.R. 4250), the Predatory Lending Consumer Protection Act

---

4. An alternative apportionment would be using the total assets as weights, since large banks are likely to pay more in dues than small ones. This does not alter the empirical results.

of 2002 (S. 2438); and the Predatory Lending Consumer Protection Act of 2001 (H.R. 1051). Once the related bills are grouped, the total number of times an individual bill or at least one of the bills in a group is listed as a specific issue of interest by either firms or associations. Based on these counts, the bills and groups of bills are ranked by "popularity." The first nineteen spots in the ranking are groups of bills; the Gramm-Leach-Bliley Act (S. 900) is the most common individual bill for which firms and associations have lobbied. There is one ranking for all of the bills and groups of bills and another for the top one hundred most common bills or groups of bills. These counts and rankings are used as weights to split the total lobbying expenditure. Essentially, the firms' lobbying expenditure is multiplied by the count and the two rank variables to produce three scaled lobbying expenditure variables.

Network Connections

To analyze the extent to which connectedness may have an influence on the legislative process or make lobbying more effective, whether and how the career paths of various legislators, lobbyists, and financial executives have crossed (the "revolving door") is documented. The primary measure of network connections captures the association between the legislators and the lobbyists working on a particular bill. The variable is measured at the legislator-bill level and uses information on the professional background of the lobbyists hired to work on that bill. The names of the lobbyists are extracted from the lobbying reports, while the information on their backgrounds is compiled from various sources, including *Washington Representatives Directory*, published by Columbia Books in its suite of www.lobbyists.info products, and GovTrack.us.

This bill-legislator level variable is defined as a dummy that equals 1 if at least one of the lobbyists working on a specific bill is connected to a particular legislator. This connection is defined either by the lobbyist having worked in that legislator's office or by the lobbyist having worked with a committee on which the legislator had a seat. Conceptually, this measure is close to the one used by Jordi Blanes-Vidal, Mirco Draca, and Christian Fons-Rosen (2012). The difference is that they look at the connections from an individual lobbyist's perspective while the variable for each bill-legislator pair is constructed by determining whether any of the lobbyists who have worked on a particular bill were employed as staffers in a specific legislator's office or on a committee associated with a specific legislator who voted on that bill.

Also used is a legislator-level variable to capture the connectedness of the legislators with Wall Street. This is a dummy that equals 1 if the legislator ever worked in FIRE (capturing the networks directly linking Wall Street to Capitol Hill). This variable is similar in spirit to the definition of connections used in Faccio (2006) and Braun and Raddatz (2009). It is possible to further distinguish this measure chronologically in an alternative construction so that it reflects whether the legislator worked in the financial industry after her time in public office. These variables are constructed using biographical information on the legislators from various sources, including GovTrack.us.

Actions

There are various points in the legislative process at which a legislator makes her stance on the proposed bill known. Obviously, recorded votes on passage constitute one such point, but as mentioned earlier, not all bills get to this final stage. For those that do (ten out of a total of forty-seven bills), the roll call records for all senators and representatives are obtained from www.voteview.com, a website maintained by Keith Poole. For bills that never make it to the final voting stage (or do but do not have recorded votes), it is important to analyze the information hidden in the earlier stages of the legislative process. Put simply, lobbying may alter the path a bill takes from the very beginning. To explore what inferences one can make based on the observations concerning these bills, data on the sponsorships and co-sponsorships, which indicate support for a bill, are gathered. The source in this case is GovTrack.us. Co-sponsorship on a bill often translates into voting in favor of that bill; Mian, Sufi, and Trebbi (2010) also use co-sponsorship information in addition to actual votes in their analysis of legislative actions related to the expansion of subprime mortgages.

Details of each of the bills are scrutinized to categorize them into two types: (1) those promoting deregulation ("lax bills") and (2) those advocating tighter regulation of the activities of the lenders ("tight bills"). The provisions of bills make such a lax-tight classification reasonably unambiguous: lax bills are those offering more options to the lenders in conducting their activities, while tight bills impose restrictions on lending activities. For example, the American Dream Downpayment Act opens the door to lower-downpayment loans, enhancing mortgage lending opportunities, whereas the Predatory Lending Consumer Protection Act introduces additional disclosure requirements and increases penalties for creditor violations. The bills are further grouped into six categories based on their similarities to reflect the fact that the bills that end up in the same "category" actually are "reincarnations" of each other. Note that each category and reincarnation pair defines an individual bill.

To explore the relationship between lobbying, connections, and the outcomes of the legislative process in a systematic manner, the actions on bills with opposite implications for the financial industry are translated into a common measure of stance on deregulation. To put it more precisely, "stance in favor of deregulation" is defined as a dummy that takes the value 1 if on the particular lax bill in question the legislator signed up as a (co-)sponsor or her vote was "aye" and 0 if she did not (co-)sponsor the bill or voted "nay."

The primary dependent variable in the empirical analysis measures the probability of a legislator switching her stance from being against to being in favor of deregulation. It is a dummy with value 1 if the legislator changed her vote from "nay" ("aye") to "aye" ("nay") on successive reincarnations of a lax (tight) bill if the bill was ultimately voted on. If the bill did not have a roll call, then the dummy is set to 1 if the legislator switched from not (co-)sponsoring a bill to (co-)sponsoring. For example, a legislator is defined as switching her stance if, say, within the category of "Predatory Lending Consumer Protection Act" she switches from being against the first reincarnation of the bill (H.R. 3901, Anti-Predatory Lending Act of 2000) to being in support of the second reincarnation of the same bill category (H.R. 4213, Consumer Mortgage Protection Act of 2000).

Mortgage Lending

Mortgage lenders are required to provide detailed information on the applications they receive and the loans they originate under the Home Mortgage Disclosure Act (HMDA), enacted by Congress in 1975. The original purpose of HMDA was twofold: to enhance enforcement of antidiscriminatory lending laws and to disseminate information to guide investments in housing.

The act requires financial institutions to disclose information to their regulatory agency about every loan application they receive. Whether an institution is covered depends on its size, the extent of its activity in a metropolitan statistical area (MSA), and the weight of residential mortgage lending in its portfolio. Any depository institution with a home office or branch in an MSA must report HMDA data if it has made a home purchase loan on a one- to four-unit dwelling or has refinanced a home purchase loan and if it has assets above an annually adjusted threshold. Any nondepository institution with at least 10 percent of its loan portfolio composed of home purchase loans must also report HMDA data if it has assets exceeding $10 million. Under these criteria, small lenders and lenders with offices only in nonmetropolitan areas are exempt from HMDA data reporting requirements. Therefore, information for rural areas tends to be incomplete. Yet, U.S. census figures show that about 83 percent of the population lived in metropolitan areas over our sample period, and hence, the bulk of residential mortgage lending activity is likely to be reported under the HMDA. Comparisons of the total number of loan originations in the HMDA and industry sources indicate that around 90 percent of mortgage lending activity is covered in this database. The information covers individual characteristics (such as race, ethnicity, income, and geographic location of the property), loan information (amount requested, response, reasons for denial, and so on), and institution information (regulatory authority, geographic location, and assets). There were about 250 million loan applications between 1996 and 2007.[5]

Although HMDA is a relatively homogeneous data set considering its size, there are some inconsistencies that need to be dealt with. To make sure that the data are clear of outliers and erroneous values, the following procedures are applied to the raw data:

- Loan amount and applicant income are rounded to a lower limit; hence, all observations below $1,000 and $10,000, respectively, are eliminated.[6]
- Numerous data validity checks operated by the FFIEC found some loan application records (LARs) to be wrong or inconsistent. Such records, after being altered automatically, have been marked as "edited," using a flag. Around 6 percent of all records are marked as edited. Edits are distributed in a homogeneous fashion across time and across space. In any event, those records have been dropped.
- All application records that did not end in one of the three following actions are eliminated: loan originated, application approved but not accepted, application denied. Other actions mostly represent dubious statuses (for example, an application withdrawn by the applicant) or purchased loans; the latter have also been excluded because it is not clear whether they are reported twice, once by the originating institution and again by the purchasing institution.
- HMDA disclosure requirements change, although minimally, from one year to the next to reflect changes in metropolitan area definitions and keep minimum institution size in line with inflation. While there is little to be done to account for the fact that the set of institutions qualifying under the applicable size restrictions changes, the observations that cannot be associated with a metropolitan area are dropped.[7]
- The year 2004 was marked by a major overhaul of the HMDA regulations. With the addition of new variables—including the interest rate when it is set above a certain threshold—the number of variables expanded from 30 to 45. Moreover, the Office of Management and Budget (OMB) increased the number of official metropolitan areas (MAs) from about 320 to about 390. The boundaries of the MAs themselves were sometimes enlarged, increasing the number of lenders required to report. Trends apparent from a comparison of aggregate figures from 2003 and 2004 therefore should be taken with a grain of salt. For example, loan market growth rates are likely to be inflated because in the existing MAs more institutions were required to disclose; at the same time, in a specific MA figures could be understated because parts of the counties that used to form it have been incorporated into a new MA. In such cases, 2004 aggregate figures have been interpolated using 2003 and 2005 figures. Definitions of applicant race, loan purpose, and purchaser type also changed between 2003 and 2004. For applicant race, an applicant ethnicity variable has been added and the race code for Hispanic has been eliminated. Other codes have been rearranged. In the construction of the data set, these variables are transformed into harmonized dummies for selected ethnicities. The loan purpose category "multifamily" was moved to a new specific variable called "property type" in 2004. To harmonize the pre-2003 and post-

---

5. The data can be ordered on CD-ROMs from the Federal Financial Institutions Examination Council (FFIEC). Starting in 2006, they could also be downloaded from the FFIEC website.

6. It is likely that some of these loans correspond to those that include "information fraud," as identified in Piskorski, Seru, and Witkin (2013).

7. These observations typically turn out to be either loans made in rural areas by institutions whose primary business is in metropolitan areas and are therefore required to report or loans that were made in an area that happened to be reclassified as rural.

2003 data, all multifamily-related records are eliminated.[8]

After these basic steps to clean and harmonize the data are taken, additional procedures can further narrow down the observations of interest for the research question at hand. In particular, to concentrate on a relatively homogeneous set of loans, it is common to drop loans for multifamily purpose from the sample, as this market is distinct from the overall mortgage market for single-family homes. Similarly, federally insured loans are often dropped, as their risk profile is likely to differ from that of other loans.

To the dismay of many researchers looking into the root causes of the 2008 financial crisis, HMDA data do not include a field that identifies whether an individual loan application is a subprime loan application.[9] An alternative way to distinguish between subprime and prime loans is using the subprime lenders list as compiled by the U.S. Department of Housing and Urban Development (HUD) each year. Since 1993, HUD has annually identified a list of lenders that specialize in either subprime or manufactured-home lending. HUD uses a number of HMDA indicators, such as origination rates, share of refinance loans, and proportion of loans sold to government-sponsored housing enterprises, to identify potential subprime lenders. Since 2004, lenders are required to identify loans for manufactured housing and loans in which the annual percentage rate (APR) on the loan exceeds the rate on the Treasury security of comparable maturity by at least three (five for second-lien loans) percentage points and report this information under HMDA. The rate spread can be used as an alternative indicator (to the HUD list) to classify subprime loans. For the years with available data, the ranking of subprime lenders using the rate spread variable alone coincides closely with the ranking in the HUD list. (The correlation is around 0.8.)

Data can then be collapsed to the MSA-lender level with 378 MSAs and almost 9,000 lenders. It is straightforward to compute several variables of interest to assess the riskiness of mortgage lending activities: loan-to-income ratios (LIRs) at origination, loan securitization rates, mortgage loan growth rate, and the extent of activity by lobbying lenders at the MSA level.

Construction of the Final Data Set

Matching Lobbying Firms to Lenders

The matching of the lobbying and HMDA databases is a tedious task that must be done manually, using company names. It starts with all the companies in the lobbying database to perform a first stage of matching with HMDA based on company names. For this purpose, an algorithm is used to find common words in lender names to narrow down the potential matches in HMDA of lenders in the lobbying database and then go through these one by one to determine the right match. Then the unmatched companies filing lobbying expense reports are manually checked one by one to mark any mergers and acquisitions (or other events) that might have induced a name change.[10] Once a list of previous and current names for each company is obtained, a second-stage matching based on an algorithm finds potential matches by searching for common words in the name strings. After the algorithm narrows down the potential matches of lobbying firms among the HMDA lenders, the list is checked one by one once again to determine the right match.

---

8. Purchaser type has also undergone a minor recoding to make room for "securitization," that is, the packaging and sale of loans on the open market, as opposed to the sale of the whole loan to a private institution or government-sponsored enterprise. No adjustments are made for this change when constructing the data set as the researchers do not distinguish between loan sales and securitized loans.

9. More generally, HMDA does not ask for information on the credit score of the borrower and the loan-to-value ratio of the property. Interestingly, an initiative to expand coverage to these areas in 2004 was fended off by financial industry efforts.

10. The manual part of the process also captures cases of a company changing its name—for example, First Equity Mortgage Bank becoming FEMBi.

To capture the full extent of the lobbying activities carried out by an entity, the corporate structure of the firms that appear in the lobbying database and might be matched to particular HMDA lenders based on the algorithm are meticulously examined. This is necessary because firms that may not be exactly the same are often linked in a corporate sense. Based on the affiliation between the lobbying company and the matches, the lobbying amounts are assigned to four different variables: amount spent by the lender itself, amount spent by the lender's parent company, amount spent by the lender's affiliates, and amount spent by the lender's subsidiary. For instance, Countrywide Financial Corp was a bank-holding company that owned Countrywide Home Loans, Inc., Countrywide Bank N.A., Countrywide Mortgage Ventures, LLC, and Countrywide Real Estate Finance. Both Countrywide Financial Corp and Countrywide Home Loans, Inc., report lobbying expenses, and all subsidiaries of Countrywide Financial Corp, but not the bank-holding company itself, file HMDA information. In this case, the lobbying expense of Countrywide Financial Corp is entered as that of the "parent" in our merged database for all the subsidiaries. The amount spent by Countrywide Home Loans, Inc., is recorded as the lender's own lobbying expense ("self"), while the same amount is entered as that of the "sister" for the other affiliates in the HMDA database. Although it is not the case in this example, it is also possible that the firm filing the lobbying expense report is a subsidiary while the parent company does not appear in the lobbying database, but only in the HMDA database. Such cases are recorded in the form of a fourth variable: the lobbying expense of the "child." If there are no parent companies, affiliates, or subsidiaries, or if the company itself does not appear in the lobbying database, the corresponding lobbying variable is set to zero. The lobbying variables used in the regressions often are a summary of these four variables.

Identifying Lobbying Activity Targeted to the Mortgage Market
The analysis distinguishes between lobbying activities that are related to mortgage market–specific issues and other lobbying activities. Concentrating only on issues related to the five general issues of interest (accounting, banking, bankruptcy, housing, and financial institutions), information is gathered on the specific issues that were listed by the lobbyists as the main issue for the lobbying activity. Then it is decided whether an issue can be directly linked to restrictions on mortgage market lending. For example, the Predatory Mortgage Lending Practices Reduction Act of 2003 (H.R. 1163) and the Fair and Responsible Lending Act of 2005 (H.R. 4471), regulating high-cost mortgages, are bills deemed to be relevant to the mortgage market. On the other hand, the Consumer Debt Prevention and Education Act of 2005 (H.R. 2201) and the Sarbanes-Oxley Act of 2002, although in general related to financial services, have no provisions directly related to mortgage lending and are not classified as mortgage market–specific issues.

After classifying all listed issues, lobbying expenditures on specific issues are calculated by splitting the total amount spent evenly across issues. To be more precise, the total lobbying expenditure is first divided by the number of all general issues and then multiplied by the number of general issues selected. Then it is divided by the total number of specific issues listed under the five general issues and multiplied by the number of specific issues of interest. Suppose firm A spends $300 and lobbies on three general issues (banking and housing, which are general issues of interest, and trade, which is not); it lists two specific issues under banking and housing (H.R. 1163, which is a relevant specific issue, and H.R. 2201, which is not relevant). In this example, the final lobbying expenditure variable is calculated as $(((300/3)*2)/2)*1 = \$100$.

Data at the Metropolitan Statistical Area Level

Despite its broad coverage on borrower, property, and loan characteristics, several important variables that might have an impact on lending decisions are left out of HMDA. The lack of knowledge of the applicant's credit score and age, the interest rate and maturity of the loan, and the property price are just examples of missing fundamental information on which the lender might base the decision.

Some of this essential information might be partially recovered through the use of economic and social indicators available for the geographical area. For that purpose, data come from the following sources:[11]

- *Bureau of Economic Analysis (BEA):* Annual data on personal income, labor and capital remuneration, proprietors' employment, and population
- *Bureau of Labor Statistics (BLS):* Data on unemployment and prices
- *U.S. Census Bureau:* Data on population
- *Office of Federal Housing Enterprise Oversight (OFHEO):* Housing price index (HPI)
- *CoreLogic LoanPerformance* (http://www.corelogic.com/): Mortgage delinquencies (the percentage of subprime loans that are sixty or more days delayed in payment) from four different points in time (February 2005, 2006, and 2007 and November 2007).[12]

FINDINGS

The empirical analysis using the data set described in the previous section documents two of the themes discussed at the beginning of the paper: the impact of political influence on financial regulation legislation, and the heightened risks taken by lobbying lenders.

Let us start by presenting some data on the overall magnitude of politically targeted spending and connections. Between 1999 and 2006, interest groups spent on average about $4.2 billion per political cycle on targeted political activity (table 1). This is the total for campaign contributions and lobbying expenditures, but it is striking that the latter represents

---

11. As mentioned earlier, the definitions of MAs change over time, both because of change in administrative standards and, more often, because of the dynamic nature of cities. OMB instituted major changes in the definitions in 2003, and HMDA incorporated them into its requirements in 2004. Hence, it is necessary to adjust the aggregation of data to reflect these changes in definitions to make sure that data are consistent pre- and post-2004. Further harmonization of metropolitan area definitions is necessary because some sources use different codes. The new codes identify physical MAs as core-based statistical areas (CBSAs). A CBSA can span more than one state but always covers counties in their entirety without splitting them. Large areas such as New York–Newark–Bridgeport (NY-NJ-CT-PA) are in turn subdivided into metropolitan divisions (MDs) in order to maintain a more comparable area size. MDs, too, are made up of whole counties. The only exception to this rule is the New England city and town areas (NECTAs) used by BLS. For historical reasons, New England city boundaries are administratively allowed to cut across counties. It is therefore impossible to match NECTA borders to CBSA and MD codes; while there are CBSA codes for Boston and other NECTAs, the Census Bureau warns that these codes represent statistical artifacts that do not match exactly the actual borders. For this reason, unemployment and inflation figures for NECTAs have been imputed without adjustment to the corresponding CBSAs (hence, at the highest level of aggregation to minimize errors). CoreLogic LoanPerformance data, excluding the November 2007 version, are expressed using the 1999 codes. At a first approximation, in the 1999 codebook CBSAs were replaced by consolidated metropolitan statistical areas (CMSAs) and MDs were replaced by primary metropolitan statistical areas (PMSAs). In order to fit PMSA-based data to our data set, the data were merged to single counties according to their former PMSA; CBSA values were then calculated by averaging the value taken by each of the counties constituting the CBSA. In this way it was possible to have a continuous and consistent series where one PMSA had been split into two CBSAs in the new codes, or vice versa. However, some of the seventy new MAs of the 2003 definition were new areas that had only recently reached the metropolitan area threshold, and therefore these areas were excluded. HMDA data always report the county where the property is located, and therefore it was possible to associate the 2003 definitions with pre-2004 data. We re-create two artificial, coherent "CBSA" and "MD" variables for the individual data in all seven years. Of course, the pre-2004 coverage of MAs created in 2004 is not complete, as local institutions were deemed to be rural and therefore not required to file under HMDA. On the other hand, a large part of lending in nonmetropolitan cities is still carried out by lenders that are required to file, so we include these observations.

12. These data provided a good set of variables to control for the usual suspects. Options to match individual loans to other data sources where credit score, interest rate, loan-to-value ratio, and so on, are available could also be considered.

Table 1. Targeted Political Activity: Campaign Contributions and Lobbying Expenditures (in Millions of Dollars), 1999–2014

	1999–2000	2001–2002	2003–2004	2005–2006	2007–2008	2009–2010	2011–2012	2013–2014
Campaign contributions	$326	$348	$461	$509	$553	$576	$602	$621
Overall lobbying expenditure	2,972	3,348	4,081	4,747	5,928	6,774	6,380	6,197
Expenditure by FIRE	437	478	645	720	854	922	939	949
Share of FIRE in overall lobbying (percent)	14.7	14.3	15.8	15.2	14.4	13.6	14.7	15.3
Total targeted political activity	$3,298	$3,696	$4,542	$5,256	$6,481	$7,349	$6,982	$6,819

Source: Author's calculations based on data from the Center for Responsive Politics.

by far the bulk of all interest groups' money spent on targeted political activity (close to 90 percent). FIRE, accounting for roughly 15 percent of overall lobbying expenditures in any election cycle, is among the most politically active industries.[13] Approximately 10 percent of all firms that lobbied during this time period were associated with FIRE. Of all 790 legislators in the data set, 14 percent were connected to Wall Street. Moreover, 32 percent of the time the lobbyist hired to work on a financial regulation bill had a connection with a legislator voting on it. Overall, connections between Wall Street and Capitol Hill are not rare occurrences, and there is enough variation in these measures for regression analysis.

Next, let us describe what has been at stake in the recent past on the financial regulation front. The focus of these intense activities was a small set of regulation proposals. In particular, when bills with the same or similar name introduced more than once were consolidated under one broad concept category, there were only six proposals that the lobbying activities of the financial industry targeted. Partially as a reflection of the legislative process, these proposals were introduced in various reincarnations, sometimes as frequently as fifteen times. Lobbying efforts on different reincarnations within a bill category were somewhat evenly distributed across time. Hence, lobbying on a particular issue was not necessarily front- or back-loaded and seemed to be quite persistent through the attempts to turn a proposal into law. In total, 47 bills were considered. In the four Congresses covered in the data set, there were 790 legislators who voted on at least one of these bills. FIRE companies hired 575 lobbyists to lobby on these bills. On average, roughly $4 million was spent on a bill. The bill with the highest lobbying spending by FIRE companies was the Responsible Lending Act of 2003 (H.R. 833), introduced in the 108th Congress as the ninth reincarnation of the Predatory Lending Consumer Protection Act. In comparison, campaign contributions to these legislators by the affected firms were minuscule—$2,000 on average. Lobbying expenditure by the "other side"—that is, the consumer organizations—was also very small (roughly $20,000) compared to the amount spent by the financial firms.

Now turning to the question of whether there is a link between political influence and legislation, we first show that, from 1999 to 2006, the outcome of bills tended to lean in a direction that was favorable to the financial industry. Based on the probability that a bill will

---

13. FIRE outspent other sectors in every year until 2006 and has closely trailed the front-runner—health care—since then.

Table 2. Legislative Outcome for Financial Regulation Bills Proposed and Discussed, 2000–2006

	Individual Bills				Bills Categorized		
Tight Bill?	Signed into Law?		Number of Bills	Tight Bill?	Signed into Law?		Number of Categories
	No	Yes			No	Yes	
No	84%	16%	32	No	40%	60%	5
Yes	100%	0%	15	Yes	100%	0%	1
Number of bills	42	5	47	Number of categories	3	3	6

Source: Igan and Mishra (2011).
Note: Bills are labeled as lax or tight based on the rules they would impose on financial institutions. On the right-hand side, bills are grouped into six categories: Commodity Futures Modernization Act, Bankruptcy Abuse Prevention and Consumer Protection Act, American Dream Downpayment Act, FHA Multifamily Housing Mortgage Loan Limit Adjustment Act, Predatory Lending Consumer Protection Act, and Financial Services Regulatory Relief Act.

ultimately be signed into law, more aggressive bills are less likely to reach the end of the legislative process. On the individual bills, no tight bill passed both chambers of Congress and was ultimately signed into law, while 16 percent of the lax bills did. This difference is even more striking when individual bills are grouped into common concept categories. Actually, the majority of lax regulation proposals (three out of five) were ultimately signed into law, whereas none of the tight regulation proposals succeeded. Perhaps even more striking is the fact that consumer protection proposals aimed at regulating predatory lending were never signed into law in spite of fifteen attempts (table 2).

Next we examine whether political influence changes legislators' behavior. The strategy is to exploit the cases in which legislators "switch" positions on a given legislation proposal and hence to use the variation in political spending by FIRE companies at the bill level and the variation in the position taken by the same legislator on the same bill in its different reincarnations.[14] The switch from being opposed to deregulation to being in favor occurred in 6 percent of the legislator-bill category-reincarnation observations. Importantly, these switch cases were not confined to a particular group of legislators or a particular bill category. In fact, the switch cases were spread across all bill categories, and 71 percent of the legislators switched at least once.[15] The baseline regression equation is:

$$S_{iBR} = \alpha L_{BR} + \beta N_{iBR} + s_i * t_c + v_B * t_c + \mu_R * t_c + \epsilon_{iBR} \quad (1)$$

where S_{iBR} is the switch in the stance of the legislator i from being against to being in favor of deregulation across successive reincarnations R of the same bill category B. Note that each pair of R and B uniquely identifies an individual bill. L_{BR} is the log of the total amount of lobbying expenditures spent on the bill by the firms that were "affected" by the bill, as revealed by their decision to engage in politically targeted activities regarding the bill. Note also that L_{BR} varies at the bill category-reincarnation level but does not vary at the legislator level,

---

14. It is important throughout to remember that the regression analysis remains descriptive and there are a series of caveats in interpreting the coefficients (discussed in detail later).

15. It is also interesting to note that there were switches in favor of deregulation even after the financial crisis.

Table 3. Political Influence and Switching in Favor of Deregulation, 2000–2006

	Full Sample	Full Sample	Unconnected Lobbyists	Connected Lobbyists	Full Sample	Full Sample	Full Sample
Lobbying	0.37*** [0.02]		0.26*** [0.02]	0.46*** [0.06]	0.38*** [0.02]	0.37*** [0.02]	
Connection		0.03*** [0.01]					
Lobbying*ideology score					0.02*** [0.01]		
Lobbying*Wall Street experience						0.02*** [0.01]	
Campaign							0.01*** [0.001]
Number of observations	32,390	32,390	21,662	10,728	31,406	32,390	32,390

Source: Author's calculations based on Igan and Mishra (2011).
Note: Dependent variable is a binary variable that is 1 if a legislator changes his vote on a particular bill in favor of deregulation (that is, from nay to aye for a lax bill and from aye to nay on a tight bill). All regressions are estimated as linear probability models and include legislator-Congress, category-Congress, and reincarnation-Congress fixed effects. Robust standard errors clustered at the legislator level are in brackets. *** denotes significance at the 1 percent level.

because the lobbying reports do not provide information on which individual legislators were contacted. Notice that, since lobbying expenditures are aggregated, any effect we find on switching could be interpreted as either the direct influence of lobbying on legislator i or the indirect influence of lobbying on legislator $j \neq i$ through strategic interaction among legislators, such as bargaining on other bills or modification to the bill in question. N_{iBR} is the connection between lobbyist and legislator, which aims to capture the network connections between the legislator and the lobbyists working on a particular bill.

The results show a statistically significant, positive association between money spent on lobbying for a particular bill and legislators switching their stance in favor of deregulation (table 3). Network connections between the legislators and the lobbyists also had an effect in securing a switch in favor of deregulation. Specifically, if the lobbyist hired to contact the legislator on a bill had an employment history connecting the lobbyist to that legislator, the likelihood that the legislator would switch her stance increased. When we investigate whether lobbying was more effective when it occurred through connected rather than unconnected lobbyists, we find that spending an extra dollar on lobbying was more effective in switching a legislator's position if the lobbyist was already connected to the legislator. The effectiveness of lobbying almost doubled when the lobbying money was spent through connected lobbyists. In other words, connected lobbyists were twice as efficient. The link between lobbying expenditures and voting patterns was also enhanced by the legislators' experience on Wall Street. In particular, lobbying was more effective in moving votes toward deregulation for legislators who were "Wall Street insiders."

We repeat the analysis using PAC contributions by affected firms instead of lobbying expenditures. While the findings are qualitatively similar, the estimated effects are much smaller in magnitude. There are two plausible explanations for the weaker links between campaign contributions and voting patterns. First, PAC contributions themselves are minuscule compared to lobbying expenditures. Second, endogeneity is potentially more of a concern because we construct this variable at the bill-legislator level. In particular, PAC contributions are targeted to particular political candidates. Hence, the affected firms may allocate their contributions based on how likely they think it is that the candidate will act in favor of deregulation once she comes into office. By comparison, lobbying expenditures are targeted at particular issues rather than particular legislators and are measured at the bill level.

In a nutshell, the analysis points to strong evidence that the likelihood of a legislator changing her stance on financial regulation proposals introduced in the run-up to the crisis was linked to lobbying efforts and network connections. In addition, the evidence suggests that spending more by hiring connected lobbyists rather than unconnected ones got the financial industry more bang for their buck.

Do these results imply that the lobbying efforts of the financial industry were "successful"? The lobbying reports do not always explicitly state the stance of the filer on a given issue—for example, whether the filer supports the passage of a bill or not. There could be financial institutions that are against deregulation: for example, lenders with more prudent standards may prefer tighter rules to suppress competition by less prudent lenders. However, if we make the plausible assumption that financial institutions are on average in favor of deregulation, our empirical results suggest that the lobbying efforts were successful in obtaining this outcome. Such an assumption indeed seems plausible since some financial institutions explicitly stated their position on certain bills: for example, Bear Stearns, in lobbying on the Mortgage Reform and Anti-Predatory Lending Act, said that it "advocated the concepts in the proposal but not the proposal."

Although our specification exploits variation in voting patterns for a given legislator on the same issue, can we interpret the findings as evidence of a causal relationship? One might argue that lobbying efforts are directed at legislators who already have a tendency to switch their stance in favor of deregulation, and that hence we may be overestimating the effect of lobbying. Several considerations ameliorate such reverse-causality concerns. First, such tendencies would be captured by the legislator and Congress fixed effects and their interactions in our empirical specification. Second, lobbying expenditures were not measured at the legislator level. The information we obtained from the lobbying reports did not include any reference to particular legislators. Hence, lobbying expenditure on a bill as a whole was unlikely to be directly influenced by the voting patterns of any specific legislator.

Similar endogeneity concerns may apply to network connections. One can argue that a lobbyist's decision to work for a particular legislator may be influenced by the legislator's tendency to switch. However, connections are determined by past employment histories and thus are not likely to be affected by voting patterns on particular regulation proposals in the future.

One can also argue that firms may be likely to hire lobbyists who are connected to legislators with a higher inclination to switch. Several factors alleviate such endogeneity concerns. First, such tendencies would be captured by the legislator and Congress fixed effects and their interactions in our empirical specification. Second, when we look at the choice of hiring lobbyists, we see a reasonable degree of persistence. Specifically, the percentage of lobbyists who worked on successive reincarnations (nth and (n-1)th reincarnations) within the same bill category was very high. For example, at least 90 percent of the lobbyists working on a reincarnation of the American Dream Downpayment Act had also worked on the previous reincarnation. Given this persistence, it would be hard to argue that firms systematically change their lobbyist-hiring patterns based on legislators' stances.

Overall, it does not seem to be the case that the tendency to switch positions on a bill determines lobbying expenditures and how connections are established, but rather that lobbying and network connections sway votes from being against to being in favor of deregulation. Yet, as mentioned earlier, it is difficult to take these relationships as indications of causation.

Given that lobbying efforts appear to have been successful in creating a deregulation-friendly financial landscape, we explore what happened to mortgage lending behavior in the run-up to the 2008 crisis (using the matched HMDA data described earlier) and to the performance of lobbying lenders during the crisis. First, we analyze the relationship between lobbying and ex ante characteristics of the loans originated. We focus on three measures of mortgage lending: loan-to-income ratios (which we consider a proxy for lending standards), the proportion of loans sold (negatively correlated with the quality of the loans originated), and mortgage loan growth rates (positively correlated with risk-taking). Controlling for unobserved lender and area characteristics as well as changes over time in the macroeconomic and local lender and borrower conditions, we find that lenders that lobbied more intensively (1) originated mortgages with higher LIRs, (2) securitized a faster-growing proportion of loans originated, and (3) had faster-growing mortgage loan portfolios (table 4).

Next, we analyze measures of the ex post performance of lobbying lenders. In particular, we explore whether, at the MSA level, delinquency rates—an indicator of loan performance—were linked to the expansion of lobbying lenders' mortgage lending. We find that the faster relative growth of mortgage loans by lobbying lenders from 2000 to 2006 was associated with higher delinquency rates in 2008. We also carry out an event study during key episodes of the financial crisis to assess whether the stocks of lobbying lenders performed differently from those of other financial institutions. We find that lobbying lenders experienced negative abnormal stock returns at the time of the failures of Bear Stearns and Lehman Brothers, but positive abnormal returns around the announcement of the bailout program. Finally, we examine the determinants of how bailout funds were distributed and find that being a lobbying lender was associated with a higher probability of being a recipient of these funds.

CONCLUDING DISCUSSION

Regulatory capture has been the subject of intense debate in the aftermath of the global financial crisis. Recent research utilizes detailed data on lobbying, legislative actions, and mortgage lending to provide promising insights into how political influence may lessen the support for tighter rules and how the ensuing lax regulatory environment may allow riskier lending practices.

The appropriate policy response depends on the true motivation for lobbying, which is extremely difficult to pin down. Specialized rent-seeking would suggest that curtailing lobbying is a socially optimal outcome. If lenders lobby to inform the policymaker and promote innovation, however, lobbying would remain a socially beneficial channel to facilitate informed decision-making.

Future research should continue to seek the answer. One direction could be expanding or more carefully exploiting lobbyists' background information to gauge the extent to which their activities correspond to their expertise. In a similar vein, the balance sheets of lobbying lenders could be examined more deeply to detect any differences between them and nonlobbying lenders in risk management practices. Another angle would be to look at outcomes in approaching the question: what do they reveal about differences in mortgage credit availability and product variety in locations where lobbying lenders dominate? Another intriguing avenue would be expanding the data set to 2009–2014. Given the post-crisis consolidation in the financial industry and the ongoing implementation of new regulations, we would expect to see rigorous lobbying activity. Indeed, table 1 suggests that FIRE activities have remained robust. What the aggregate data cannot tell us, however, is if and how the incumbent survivors have changed strategies. For instance, as rule-making under the Dodd-Frank Act continues, we could expect to see lobbying shifting from Congress to regulatory agencies.

Table 4. Lobbying on Financial Regulation Bills and Mortgage Risk Taking, 2000–2006

	Loan-to-Income Ratio	Loan-to-Income Ratio	Proportion of Loans Sold	Loan Growth	Delinquency	Abnormal Returns			Bailout Funds Received
						Market Turmoil	Bailout Announcement		
Lender lobbies	0.14*** [0.01]					−0.28** [0.12]	0.30*** [0.11]		0.07*** [0.02]
Lobbying		0.004*** [0.000]	0.007*** [0.000]	0.31*** [0.09]					
Growth in market share of lobbying lenders					0.22* [0.12]				
Number of observations	648,938	648,938	406,035	406,996	306	67	45		13,315

Source: Author's calculations based on Igan, Mishra, and Tressel (2011).

Regressions where the dependent variable is the loan-to-income ratio, proportion of loans sold, and loan growth are at the lender-MSA-year level and include a full set of fixed effects. Regression where the dependent variable is delinquency is at the MSA-year level and includes a full set of fixed effects. Regressions where the dependent variable is abnormal returns or bailout funds are at the lender level and include a set of controls (log assets, dummy if regulator is HUD, dummy if lender is subprime, mortgage loan share, average income of loan applicant, average LIR of loans originated). "Market turmoil" refers to the Lehman Brothers bankruptcy, and "bailout announcement" refers to the Troubled Asset Relief Program. Robust, clustered standard errors are in brackets. ***, **, and * denote significance at the 1, 5, and 10 percent level, respectively.

While expanding our knowledge, it is important to remember that economics is ultimately about (at times irrational) human behavior and that modeling people and their decisions as inanimate objects has its limits and even perils.

REFERENCES

Acemoglu, Daron. 2009. "The Crisis of 2008: Structural Lessons for and from Economics." January 6. Available at: http://economics.mit.edu/files/3703 (accessed August 9, 2016).

Agarwal, Sumit, Efraim Benmelech, Nittai Bergman, and Amit Seru. 2012. "Did the Community Reinvestment Act (CRA) Lead to Risky Lending?" Working Paper 18609. Cambridge, Mass.: National Bureau of Economic Research (December).

Blanes-Vidal, Jordi, Mirco Draca, and Christian Fons-Rosen. 2012. "Revolving Door Lobbyists." *American Economic Review* 102(6): 3731–48.

Bonica, Adam. 2016. "A Data-Driven Voter Guide for U.S. Elections: Adapting Quantitative Measures of the Preferences and Priorities of Political Elites to Help Voters Learn About Candidates." February 24. Available at SSRN: http://ssrn.com/abstract=2742094 or http://dx.doi.org/10.2139/ssrn.2742094 (accessed August 9, 2016).

Braun, Mattias, and Claudio Raddatz. 2009. "Banking on Politics." World Bank Policy Research Working Paper Series 4902.

Calomiris, Charles. 2009. "The Subprime Turmoil: What's Old, What's New, and What's Next." *Journal of Structured Finance* 15(1): 6–52.

Faccio, Mara. 2006. "Politically Connected Firms." *American Economic Review* 96(1): 369–86.

Igan, Deniz, and Prachi Mishra. 2011. "Three's Company: Wall Street, Capitol Hill, and K Street." Unpublished paper. International Monetary Fund, Washington.

Igan, Deniz, Prachi Mishra, and Thierry Tressel. 2011. "A Fistful of Dollars: Lobbying and the Financial Crisis." *NBER Macroeconomics Annual* 26.

Johnson, Simon. 2009. "The Quiet Coup." *The Atlantic* (May).

Mian, Atif, Amir Sufi, and Francesco Trebbi. 2010. "The Political Economy of the U.S. Mortgage Default Crisis." *American Economic Review* 100(5): 1967–98.

Piskorski, Tomasz, Amit Seru, and James Witkin. 2013. "Asset Quality Misrepresentation by Financial Intermediaries: Evidence from RMBS Market." *Journal of Finance* 70(6): 2635–78.

Data Science and Political Economy: Application to Financial Regulatory Structure

SHARYN O'HALLORAN, SAMEER MASKEY, GERALDINE MCALLISTER, DAVID K. PARK, AND KAIPING CHEN

The development of computational data science techniques in natural language processing and machine learning algorithms to analyze large and complex textual information opens new avenues for studying the interaction between economics and politics. We apply these techniques to analyze the design of financial regulatory structure in the United States since 1950. The analysis focuses on the delegation of discretionary authority to regulatory agencies in promulgating, implementing, and enforcing financial sector laws and overseeing compliance with them. Combining traditional studies with the new machine learning approaches enables us to go beyond the limitations of both methods and offer a more precise interpretation of the determinants of financial regulatory structure.

Keywords: big data, natural language processing, machine learning, political economics, financial regulation, banking and financial services sector

The development of computational techniques to analyze large and complex information, or big data, opens a window to studying the interaction between economics and politics. Natural language processing (NLP) and machine learning (ML) algorithms offer new approaches to examining intricate processes such as government's regulation of markets. For example, traditional observational studies of the design of regulatory structure rely on thousands of hours of well-trained annotators coding laws to extract information on the delegation of decision-making authority to agencies, the administrative procedures that circumscribe this authority, the scope of regulation, the subsequent rules promulgated, and the impact on financial market participants. Using big data methods to analyze this predominantly text-based information reduces the time and expense of data collection and improves the validity and efficiency of estimates. Fast and accurate processing of complex information in real time enables decision-makers to evaluate alternative theories of regulatory structure and, ultimately, to predict which institutional arrangements lead to more efficient markets and under what conditions.

Big data methods undoubtedly equip researchers with tools to study political economy questions that could not be addressed previously. As we have witnessed, however, the term "big data" has been thrust into the zeitgeist in

---

Sharyn O'Halloran is George Blumenthal Professor of Political Economy and professor of international and public affairs at Columbia University. **Sameer Maskey** is assistant professor at Columbia University. **Geraldine McAllister** is Senate director at Columbia University. **David K. Park** is dean of Strategic Initiatives at Columbia University. **Kaiping Chen** is a doctoral student at Stanford University.

Direct correspondence to: Sharyn O'Halloran at so33@columbia.edu, Department of Political Science, Columbia University, 420 West 118th St., New York, NY 10027; Sameer Maskey at smaskey@cs.columbia.edu, Geraldine McAllister at gam2116@columbia.edu, David K. Park at dkp7@columbia.edu; and Kaiping Chen at kpchen23 @stanford.edu.

recent years with no consistent meaning or framework for interpreting results. Indeed, many computational analysts view big data as synonymous with causal inference: correlation supplants the need for explanation. As Rocío Titiunik (2015) explains, however, increasing the number of observations or variables in a data set does not resolve causation.[1]

We have always had "data," and lots of it. So what is different about big data today? What is new this time around can be summarized along three dimensions: granularity, real time, and textual pattern recognition. With computational advances in the data sciences, researchers can now go beyond keyword searches and use more sophisticated word sequencing to construct measures, thereby reducing error and potential bias (Lewis 2014). Why is this important? Many public policy decisions rely on temporaneous data to predict impact and mitigate potential unintended consequences. Data science techniques thereby facilitate the management and processing of large quantities of information at rapid speeds, the availability of which can lead to better-informed policy.

The purpose of this paper is to illustrate how these new computational data science methods can enhance political economy research. We apply these tools to analyze the design of financial regulatory structure in the United States since 1950. The centerpiece of this work is a large database encoding the text of financial regulation laws. Among other variables, we code the amount of regulatory authority delegated to executive agencies and the procedural constraints associated with the use of that authority. The analysis requires aggregating measures from thousands of pages of text-based data sources with tens of thousands of provisions, containing millions of words. Such a large-scale data project is time-consuming, expensive, and subject to potential measurement error. To mitigate these limitations and demonstrate the robustness of the coding procedures, we employ data science techniques to complement the observational study of financial regulatory structure. The computational analyses conducted: (1) enable sensitivity analysis around manual rules-based coding, (2) identify the magnitude and location of potential error, and (3) allow for benchmarking. The results indicate that, while the manual coding rules perform better than unstructured text alone, the accuracy of the estimates improves significantly when both methods are combined. Thus, our results underscore the complementarities of computational sciences and traditional social sciences (rules-based coding) methods when examining important political economy questions.

The first section of the paper surveys the literature on delegation and agency design, highlighting the role of uncertainty and conflict as key determinants of regulatory architecture. The central hypothesis derived from this literature is that the closer the policy preferences of Congress and the executive, the more discretionary authority is delegated to agencies. To empirically test this hypothesis, the subsequent section details the rules and criteria used to construct the financial regulatory structure database. The statistical analysis reaffirms the political nature of financial market regulation: the closer the policy preferences of Congress and the executive, the more discretionary authority is delegated. To check the robustness of these findings, we recode the financial regulation laws using NLP, which converts the text into machine-readable form. We then apply both a naive and naive Bayes model to compare three coding schemes to predict agency discretion, noting that combined methods perform best. We conclude with a discussion of the implications of incorporating computational methods into text-based coding to improve the validity and robustness of the findings.

DELEGATION, DISCRETION, AND FINANCIAL REGULATORY DESIGN

As a necessary preamble, this section reviews the literature on delegation and agency design. The extensive corpus of work on the delegation of policymaking authority to administrative

---

1. William R. Clark and Matt Golder (1995) review additional pitfalls of computational analysis, such as sampling populations, confounding variables, over-identification, and multiple hypothesis testing. See the symposium in the January 2015 issue of *PS*.

agencies can usefully be separated along three lines. First, why does Congress delegate regulatory authority? Second, how does Congress constrain agency decision-making, if at all? And third, given the answers to questions one and two, what drives the amount of substantive discretionary authority delegated by Congress?

The first strand of thought analyzes Congress's motivation to transfer authority to administrative agencies, noting key factors such as workload, political risk, bureaucratic expertise, and interest group politics, to name but a few. The aim of this line of inquiry is to describe, and at times even rationalize, the explosive growth of the federal bureaucracy and the corresponding implications for democratic institutions.[2] A second and related line of reasoning questions the constitutionality of Congress delegating expansive legislative authority to unelected bureaucrats. It contends that such unconstrained authority equates to congressional abrogation of its policymaking responsibilities and thereby fundamentally undermines the U.S. system of separate powers.[3] The counterpoint to these assertions recognizes that while Congress grants administrative functions to professional bureaucrats for many legitimate reasons, it would be foolhardy for reelection-minded legislators to hand over policy prerogatives without checks on agency action. Instead, when designing regulatory agencies, Congress specifies the criteria, rules, and administrative procedures that govern bureaucratic behavior. While this is not a perfect solution to the ubiquitous principal-agent problems of oversight and control (for example, bureaucratic drift), legislators can nonetheless retain both ex ante and ex post control over policy outcomes.[4]

Building upon the insights of these first two bodies of research, a growing literature recognizes that regulatory structure reflects the dynamics of an underlying principal-agent problem between Congress and the bureaucracy. Here the question shifts from why and how Congress delegates to what drives legislators' decision to give agencies substantive discretion in setting policy. What factors motivate Congress's choice? David Epstein and Sharyn O'Halloran (1999) show that more delegation occurs when Congress and the executive have aligned preferences, policy uncertainty is low, and the cost of Congress making policy itself is high. A recurring theme in much of the new political economy literature on agency design is that this conflict arises because of a downstream moral hazard problem between the agency and the regulated firm: that is, there is uncertainty over policy outcomes. Agency structure is thereby endogenous to the political environment in which it operates.[5] This trade-off between distributive losses and informational gains is further elaborated in a series of studies examining the politics of delegation with an executive veto (Volden 2002), civil service protections for bureaucrats (Gailmard and Patty 2007, 2012), and executive review of proposed regulations (Wiseman 2009), among others.[6]

The application of these models to the regulation of banking and financial services would seem to be well motivated. Banking is certainly a complex area where bureaucratic expertise would be valuable; Donald Morgan (2002), for instance, shows that rating agencies disagree significantly more over banks and insurance companies than over other types of firms. Furthermore, continual innovation in

---

2. For examples of this logic, see Stigler (1971), Fiorina (1977, 1982), and McCubbins (1985).

3. This view is articulated most clearly by Lowi (1979), Moe (1984), and Sundquist (1981).

4. See, for example, McCubbins and Schwartz (1984) and McCubbins, Noll, and Weingast (1987, 1989).

5. Some excellent technical work has been done on the optimal type of discretion to offer agencies. Nahum D. Melumad and Toshiyuki Shibano (1991) and Ricardo Alonso and Niko Matouschek (2008) provide instances where a principal would prefer to offer a menu of discontinuous choices to an agent receiving authority. Sean Gailmard (2009) demonstrates, however, that in situations where the principal cannot precommit to certain courses of action, interval-type delegation regimes are optimal.

6. See also Bendor and Meirowitz (2004) for contributions to the spatial model of delegation and Volden and Wiseman (2011) for an overview of the development of this literature.

the financial sector causes older regulations to become less effective, or "decay," over time. If it did not delegate authority in this area, Congress would have to continually pass new legislation to deal with the new forms of financial firms and products, which it has shown neither the ability nor inclination to do.

These insights also overlap with the economic literature on the location of policymaking, as in Maskin and Tirole (2004) and Alesina and Tabellini (2007), both of which emphasize the benefits of delegation to bureaucrats or other non-accountable officials (such as courts) when presented with technical policy issues about which the public would have to pay high costs to become informed. We also draw parallels with the work of Yolande Hiriart and David Martimort (2012), who study the regulation of risky markets and show that when firms cannot be held individually responsible for the consequences of their actions, ex post regulators are faced with the ex ante moral hazard problem of firms engaging in overly risky behavior. Finally, we draw inspiration from agency-based models of corporate finance, as summarized in Tirole (2006).

Overall, then, we have the following testable hypotheses:[7]

1. *Allied principle:* Congress delegates more discretion when:
   a. The preferences of the president and Congress are more similar; and
   b. Uncertainty over market outcomes (moral hazard) is higher.
2. *Uncertainty principle:* The more risk-averse is Congress:
   a. The higher is the overall level of discretion; and
   b. The higher is the level of market regulation.

FINANCIAL REGULATORY STRUCTURE: AN OBSERVATIONAL STUDY

The logic and predictions derived from the theoretical literature described in the previous section inform the research design that we adopted and the subsequent financial regulation database that we constructed. Traditional methods used to test hypotheses rely on observational data to measure the dependent variable, such as financial regulatory structure, and the independent variables, such as differences in policy preferences, to make inferences regarding probable effect. The benefits of this research design are numerous; researchers can: (1) translate a model's theoretical propositions into testable hypotheses; (2) specify the mechanisms by which one variable impacts another; and (3) falsify hypotheses generated by alternative models. This exercise places theoretical arguments within an empirical context, highlighting important factors and thereby contributing to building better theory.

Two main challenges arise with observational studies: precision and validity.[8] To improve the precision of our estimates and mitigate any potential random error generated by compounding effects, we hold constant the issue area, focusing on financial regulatory structure, and employ multiple methods to check the robustness of our measures.[9] To improve the validity of our findings, we compare the current results with a cross-sectional study of all significant laws over the same time period.[10]

Constructing a Financial Regulation Database

Although many excellent histories of financial regulation are available,[11] and despite the popular argument that deregulation of the financial sector played a key role in the recent economic crisis, there is as yet no measure of

---

7. For detail proofs of these propositions, see Groll, O'Halloran, and McAllister (2014).

8. Melissa D.A. Carlson and R. Sean Morrison (1999) define "precision" as the lack of random error or random variation in a study's estimates. "Validity" refers to the extent to which the findings of a study can be generalized.

9. By analyzing a single issue area, we control for the variance in market uncertainty and downstream (moral hazard) risks.

10. Here we reference the work of Epstein and O'Halloran (1999).

11. Here we reference the work of Epstein and O'Halloran (1999).

financial regulatory structure over time.¹² To test the hypotheses that agency discretion responds to the political preferences of Congress and the executive, we therefore created a new database comprising all federal laws and agency rules enacted from 1950 to 2009 that regulate the financial sector.¹³

The unit of analysis is an individual law regulating financial markets. While distinctions between the different types of financial institutions have become blurred over time, for the purposes of this research we define the universe of finance and financial institutions to include state-chartered and federally chartered banks, bank holding companies, thrifts and savings and loan associations, credit unions, investment banks, financial holding companies, securities, broker dealers, commodities, and mortgage lending institutions.

Sample Selection Criteria
Following David Mayhew (2005), we identify the relevant legislation in a three-sweep process. First, we include all laws mentioned in the policy tracker of the relevant issues of *Congressional Quarterly Almanac* (*CQ*) for the categories of banking, the savings and loan industry, the Federal Reserve, the stock market and financial services, insurance, and mortgages, yielding 69 laws. In the second sweep, we review the relevant secondary literature, such as *Banking Law and Regulation* (Macey, Miller, and Carnell 2001), reports by the Congressional Research Service, the websites of the federal banking regulators, and "Legislation in Current Congress" at the Library of Congress's THOMAS website. Any laws not already identified in the first sweep are included, thereby expanding our list by 81 additional laws. In the third sweep, we compare our list of key legislation against John Lapinski's (2008) 1,000 most significant U.S. laws to ensure that our sample covers all critical pieces of financial regulation legislation. Here we add another 5 laws. This process brings the total number of laws in our sample to 155. As our analysis focuses on regulatory design, we omit the mortgage lending laws, resulting in a sample size of 112 financial regulation laws.

The primary source for coding each law is *CQ*'s year-end summary of major legislation (80 laws). When data prove unavailable from *CQ*, we refer to the Library of Congress's THOMAS database (27 laws). When neither source contains sufficient detailed information on a specific law, we refer to the U.S. Statutes (5 laws). In omnibus legislation with a financial regulation subpart, we code only the relevant provisions (9 cases). Each law is then classified as belonging to one or more categories: depository institutions, securities, commodities, insurance, interest rate controls, consumer protection, mortgage lending or government-sponsored enterprises, and state-federal issues.

As a first cut into the analysis, the distribution of financial regulation laws by Congress is illustrated in figure 1, with unified and divided governments shown. At first blush, the figure does not indicate the influence of partisan factors in passing financial legislation; the average number of laws per Congress is almost identical under periods of unified and divided government.

Coding Discretion
Agency discretion depends on both the authority delegated and the associated limits on its

---

12. In a recent study of wages in the financial sector over time, Thomas Philippon and Ariell Reshef (2009) developed an index of deregulation, built around summary measures of bank branching restrictions, the separation of commercial and investment banks, interest rate ceilings, and the separation of banks and insurance companies. Unfortunately, their measure codes only for *deregulation* and omits the potential for increases in market regulation as witnessed in the Dodd-Frank Wall Street Reform and Consumer Protection Act of 2010 (P.L. 111-203). In contrast, we analyze the political and economic determinants of regulatory structure and the subsequent impact on the financial sector. For a detailed discussion of Philippon and Reshef's measure, see the data appendix.

13. The analysis begins in 1950 because in that year *Congressional Quarterly* started providing consistent reviews of the key provisions of enacted legislation. The major data sets compiled for the financial regulation database are summarized in the data appendix, which also provides the step-by-step manual coding process.

Figure 1. Financial Bills Passed per Congress, 1950–2009

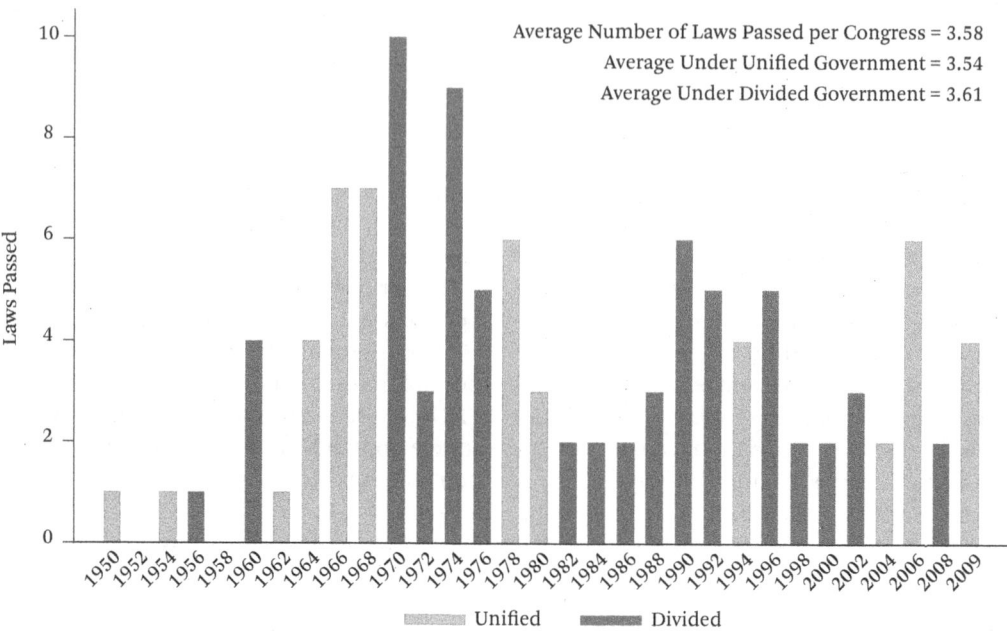

Source: Authors' compilation.

use. Therefore, for each law we code for whether substantive authority is granted to executive agencies, the agency receiving authority (for example, the Securities and Exchange Commission [SEC], the Commodity Futures Trading Commission [CFTC], or the U.S. Treasury), and the location of the agency within the administrative hierarchy (for example, the Executive Office of the President, the cabinet, or an independent agency).

We then identify the procedural constraints circumscribing agency actions.[14] These data provide the bases from which we calculate law-by-law agency discretion.[15]

Delegation is defined as authority granted to an executive branch actor to move policy away from the status quo.[16] To measure delegation, then, we read each law in our database independently, number its provisions, and identify and count all provisions that delegate substantive authority to the executive branch. From these tallies, we calculate the delegation

---

14. Additionally, we collect the number of regulatory agencies delegated authority per law; this shows the degree to which authority is being divided across executive branch actors. Regulators' degree of autonomy is measured by the relative mix of independent regulatory actors receiving authority, as opposed to actors and executive agencies under more direct presidential control. Each law is also coded for whether it increases, decreases, or leaves unchanged the regulatory stringency of financial markets based on disclosure rules, capital requirements, or increased oversight of products and firms. This enables us to construct a regulation-deregulation index, beginning in 1950 and running to 2010. Table 7 in the data appendix provides descriptive statistics on the key variables used in the analysis.

15. To ensure the reliability of our measures, each law is coded independently by two separate annotators and reviewed by a third independent annotator, who notes inconsistencies. We then check each law a fourth and final time upon final entry. The data appendix provides a detailed description of the coding method used in the analysis.

16. For example, the Dodd-Frank Act delegated authority to the Federal Deposit Insurance Corporation (FDIC) to provide for an orderly liquidation process for large, failing financial institutions. See P.L. 111-203, section 210; 124 Stat 1460.

Figure 2. Histogram of Delegation Ratio

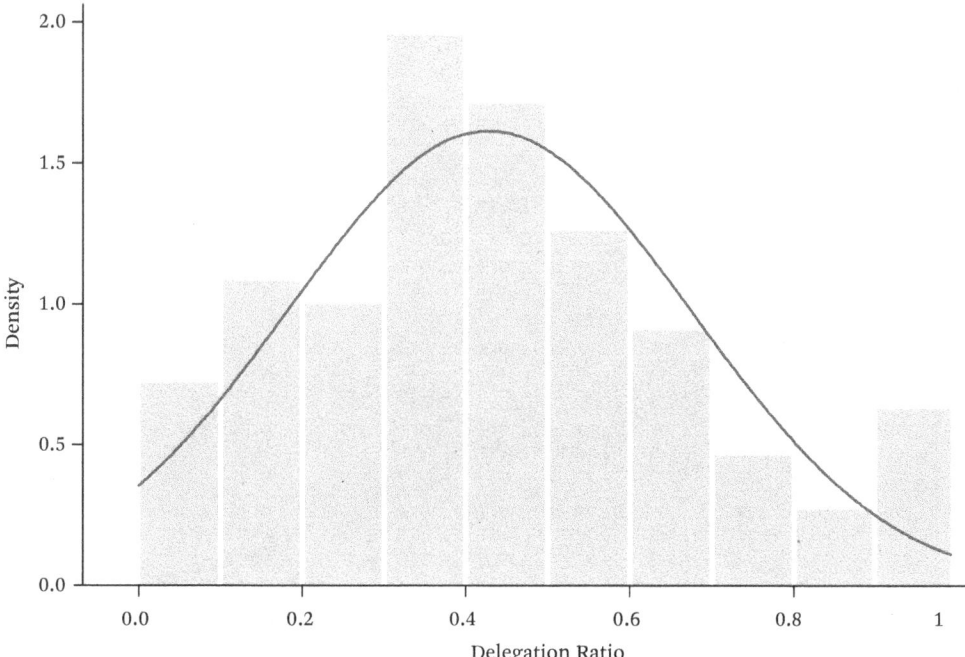

Source: Authors' compilation.

ratio by dividing the number of provisions that delegate to the executive over the total number of provisions. A histogram of delegation ratios is shown in figure 2. As indicated, the distribution follows a more or less normal pattern, with a slight spike for those laws with 100 percent delegation. (These usually have a relatively small number of provisions.)

Executive discretion depends not only on the amount of authority delegated but also on the administrative procedures that constrain executive actions.[17] Accordingly, we identify fourteen distinct procedural constraints associated with the delegation of authority and note every time one appears in a law.[18] Including all fourteen categories in our analysis would be unwieldy, so we investigated the feasibility of using principal components analysis to analyze the correlation matrix of the constraint categories. Since only one factor was significant, we calculate first-dimension factor scores for each law, convert them to the [0,1] interval, and term these the "constraint index." Figure 3 displays the histogram of constraints present in each law: the majority of the laws contain four or fewer constraint categories.

From these data, we calculate an overall "discretion index." For a given law, if the delegation ratio is D and the constraint index is C, both lying between 0 and 1, then discretion is defined as $D * (1 - C)$.[19] The more discretion an agency has to set policy, the greater the leeway it has to regulate market participants. Lower levels of agency discretion are associated with less regulation. Total discretion is thereby defined as delegation minus con-

---

17. See McCubbins, Noll, and Weingast (1987).

18. Each of these categories is coded as constraints above and beyond those required by the 1946 Administrative Procedure Act. For a detailed description of these administrative constraints and their definition, see the data appendix.

19. See Epstein and O'Halloran (1999) for a complete discussion of this measure.

Figure 3. Histogram of Constraints per Law

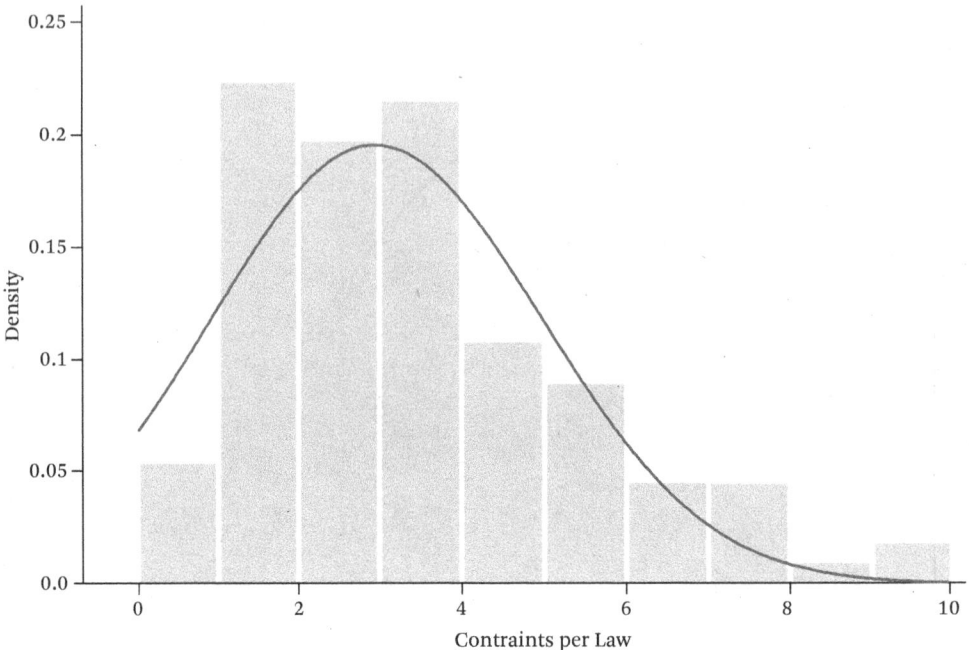

Source: Authors' compilation.

straints—that is, the amount of unconstrained authority delegated to executive actors.

To verify the robustness of our estimates and confirm that our choice of aggregation methods for constraints does not unduly impact our discretion measure, figure 4 shows the average discretion index each year calculated four different ways. Since the time series patterns are almost identical, the fourth method (continuous factors, first dimension) is not crucial to the analysis that follows.

Trends in Agency Discretion

As a basic check on our coding of delegation and regulation, we compare the distribution of the discretion index for laws that regulate the financial industry overall and laws that deregulate it. We would expect from hypothesis 2 that laws regulating the industry would delegate more discretionary authority, and figure 5 shows that this is indeed the case. The average discretion index for the thirty-one laws that deregulate is 0.29, as opposed to 0.36 for the eighty-five laws that regulate. (Five laws neither regulate nor deregulate the industry but rather clarify or qualify a provision in an earlier law.)

These trends pose a puzzle: why was there a strong regulatory response to the spate of financial innovation in the 1960s, a decade that saw an explosion of credit in the economy, including the widespread use of credit cards, accompanied by an increase in the number of credit bureaus (which were unregulated), increased use of computers, and significant growth in both the number and membership of federal credit unions, but no such response to the most recent innovations—derivatives, nonbank lenders, and the rise of the shadow banking system? Both episodes developed under divided government, after all. We return to this question later.

Figure 4 also indicates that the trend in recent decades has been for Congress to give executive branch actors less discretion in financial regulation. Since the Great Society era of the 1960s, and then on into the early 1970s, the total amount of new executive branch authority to regulate the financial sector has generally declined. The exceptions have been a few up-

Figure 4. Four Measures of Executive Discretion

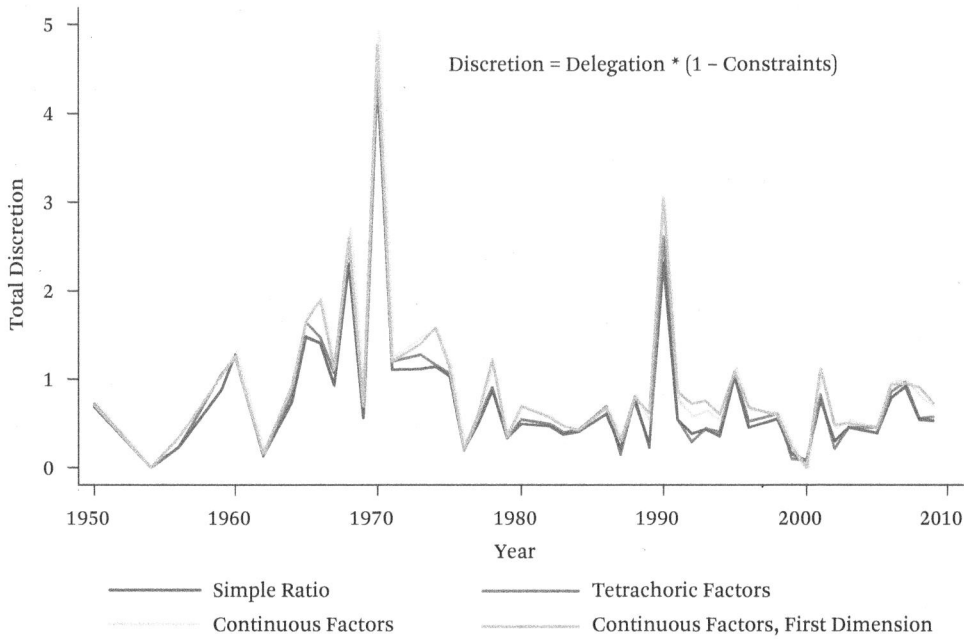

Source: Authors' compilation.

Figure 5. Distribution of Discretion Index for Deregulatory Laws and Regulatory Laws

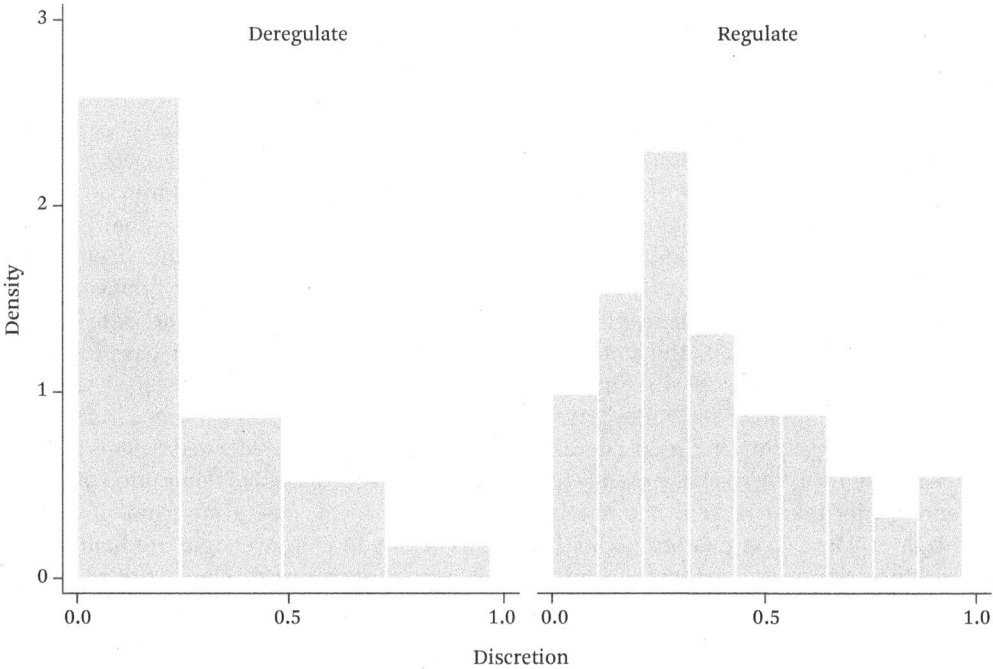

Source: Authors' compilation.

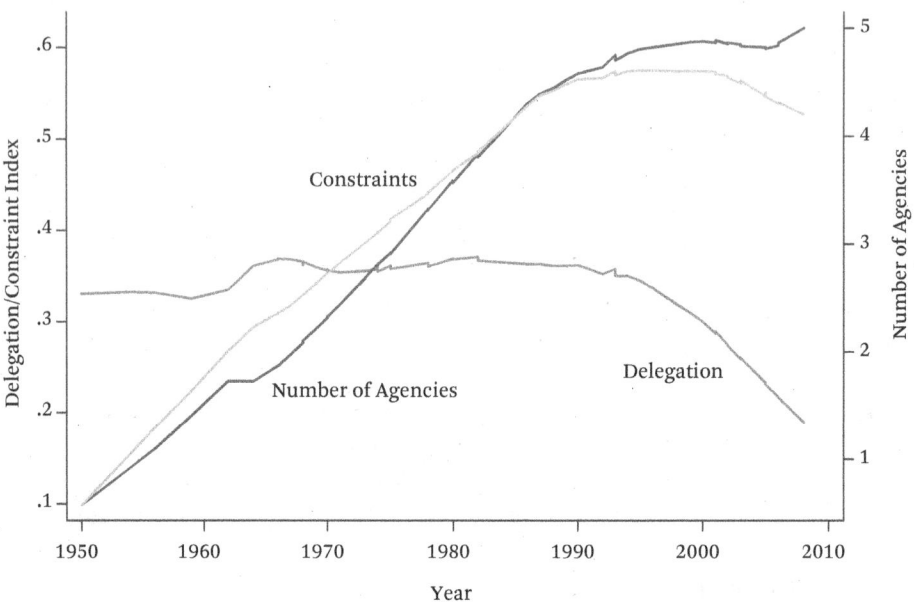

Figure 6. Delegation, Constraints, and Agencies Receiving Authority, 1950–2008

Source: Authors' compilation.

ticks in discretion that coincided with the aftermaths of well-publicized financial crises and scandals, including the savings and loan crisis of the 1980s and 1990s, the Asian crisis of the late 1990s, and the Enron scandal of 2001. Otherwise, the government has been given steadily less authority over time to regulate financial firms, even as innovations in that sector have made the need for regulation greater than ever and even as the importance of the financial sector in the national economy has greatly increased.[20]

What is the source of this decrease in discretion? As shown in figure 6, the amount of authority delegated to oversee the financial sector has remained fairly constant over time, perhaps decreasing slightly in the past decade. The trend in figure 4, then, is due mainly to a large and significant increase in the number of constraints placed on regulators' use of this authority. In addition, we find that the number of actors receiving authority has risen significantly over the time period studied, as also shown in figure 6, and that the location of these agencies in the executive hierarchy has changed, away from more independent agencies to those more directly under the president's control.

Overall, then, our preliminary analysis suggests that the current rules defining financial regulatory structure has created a web of interlocking and conflicting mandates, making it difficult for regulators to innovate in the rules and standards governing the financial industry, while at the same time opening up regulatory agencies to industry lobbying. The problem is not that there is too little regulation, then, but that regulators have too little discretion. Modern laws delegate less, constrain more, and split authority across more agencies than their predecessors. This has led to the heavy regulation of many areas of financial activity by the federal government even as those charged with oversight are hamstrung by overlapping jurisdictions, the need for other actors to sign off on their policies, or outright prohibitions on regulatory actions by Congress.

---

20. The size of the financial services sector as a percentage of GDP rose from 3 percent in 1950 to over 8 percent in 2008.

Figure 7. Partisan Effects Captured by Divided Government (Top) and by Cross-Party Coalitions (Bottom)

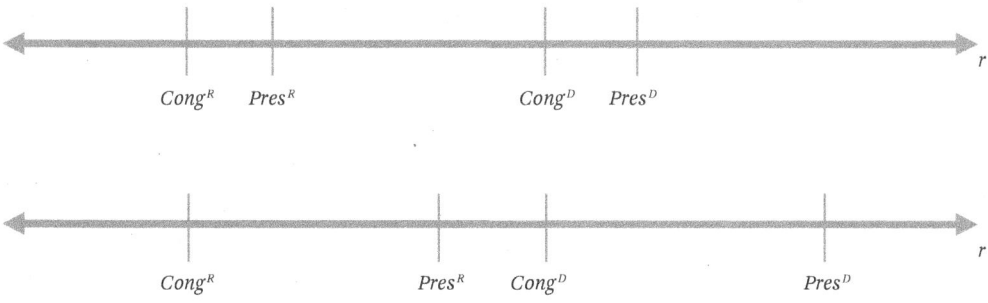

Source: Authors' compilation.

Analyzing the Financial Regulation Database

Having constructed the financial regulatory structure database, we can now test the comparative statics hypothesis generated from the theoretical literature proposing that Congress delegates greater levels of discretionary authority to executive branch actors with preferences closer to their own. As James Barth, Gerard Caprio, and Ross Levine (2006) report, policymaking in financial regulation tends to be unidimensional, separating actors with more pro-industry preferences from those who place more emphasis on consumer protection.

In the United States over the period studied, Republicans have represented the former viewpoint and Democrats the latter.[21] We also posit that presidents will tend to be less pro-industry than legislators, as their national constituency would lead them to weigh more heavily consumer interests and the stability of the banking system at large.

As figure 7 shows, however, two patterns of delegation are consistent with these constraints. If partisan differences are stronger than interbranch differences, as in the top panel, then delegation should be higher under unified government as opposed to divided government; this was the pattern of delegation found in Epstein and O'Halloran (1999). If interbranch differences predominate, however, as in the bottom panel, then delegation will actually be highest from a Democratic Congress to a Republican president, lowest from a Republican Congress to a Democratic president, and intermediate for the other two combinations. Furthermore, in this "cross-party coalition" case, delegation should increase when Congress is controlled by Democrats, as opposed to Republicans, and when the presidency is controlled by Republicans, as opposed to Democrats.

We thus have the particular prediction that, when regressing discretion on partisan control of the branches, we should obtain a positive and significant coefficient on Democratic control of Congress and Republican control of the presidency. Further, hypothesis 2 predicts that the level of market regulation will also respond to partisan control of Congress: it should increase when Democrats control Congress, as opposed to Republicans, but the party controlling the presidency may or may not matter.

The estimation results are given in table 1. The cross-party partisan conflict variable is constructed to equal 1 when Republicans control Congress and Democrats control the presidency, –1 when Democrats hold Congress and the president is Republican, and 0 otherwise. As predicted, this variable is consistently negative and significant in predicting discretion, while the usual divided government variable is not significant. The signs on Democratic control of Congress and the presidency are also as predicted, as shown in model 3, and the cross-party effects holding constant a number of control variables are added to the regression in model 4.

Models 5 and 6 indicate that when predict-

---

21. This is consistent with the findings of Kroszner and Strahan (1999), who analyze roll call votes on bank branching deregulation.

Table 1. Regression Analysis

	Discretion (1)	Discretion (2)	Discretion (3)	Discretion (4)	Regulation/ Deregulation (5)	Regulation/ Deregulation (6)
Cross-party	−0.084 (0.029)***			−0.080 (0.037)**		
Divided		0.043 (0.039)				
Democratic president			−0.066 (0.037)*		−0.573 (0.283)**	−0.637 (0.712)
Democratic congress			0.065 (0.024)***		0.764 (0.173)***	1.546 (0.566)***
Start of term				0.041 (0.042)		
Activist mood				0.012 (0.048)		
Budget deficit				0.027 (0.320)		
Δ DJIA				0.077 (0.133)		
Observations	121	121	121	108	121	23
R squared	0.071	0.011	0.091	0.074	0.169	0.425

Source: Authors' compilation.
Notes: Models 1–4 are OLS regressions with discretion as the independent variable. Models 5 and 6 are ordered probits with regulation/deregulation as the dependent variable. In model 6, only those laws with discretion indices under 0.2 are included in the sample.

ing whether a given law will regulate, deregulate, or leave unchanged the level of regulation of the financial industry, the coefficient on partisan control of Congress is significant in all cases, and in the predicted direction. The coefficient on control of the executive is significant in model 5 as well. Model 6 includes only those cases with a discretion index of 0.2 or under, as the regulation/deregulation relationship should hold most clearly when Congress does not delegate to the executive. Indeed, in these cases the coefficient on Congress remains positive and significant, while the coefficient on control of the presidency is no longer significant.[22]

Limitations of the Observational Method

The above analysis adopts a research design based on observational methods, which potentially suffer from a number of well-known shortcomings. First, observational studies assume that all variables of interest can be measured. For example, the analysis posits that discretion can be calculated as a combination of delegation and constraints. In constructing these measures, the coding rules invariably im-

---

22. These results explain the different responses to financial sector innovation mentioned earlier. In the late 1960s and early 1970s, Congress was controlled by a Democratic majority and a Republican, Nixon, held the presidency. This is the cross-party scenario (bottom panel of figure 7) that leads to greater levels of agency discretion and therefore increases in market regulation. In contrast, during the late 1990s and the first decade of the twenty-first century, the Republicans controlled Congress in all but two of the twelve years, while the parties split control of the presidency. In this scenario, the cross-party effect would predict little or no discretion delegated to agencies.

pose a structure on the text, designating some words or phrases as delegation and others as constraints. Moreover, collecting original data is extremely time-consuming, especially when derived from disparate text-based sources, as we do here. The resources needed to extract the appropriate information, train annotators, and code the data can prove prohibitive and are prone to error.

Second, standard econometric techniques, upon which many political economic studies rely, including the one conducted here, face difficulty in analyzing high-dimensional variables that could theoretically be combined in a myriad of ways. For example, figure 4 shows four possible alternatives to calculate the discretion index by varying the weights assigned to the different categories of procedural constraints.

Third, amalgamating the panoply of independent variables into a single index would miss the embedded dimensional structure of the data. For example, rooted in the discretion index are measures of delegation and constraints. Embedded in the delegation ratio and constraint index are additional dimensions: the delegation ratio is a cube formed by the number of provisions that delegate authority to the executive over the total number of provisions; the constraint index is a fourteen-sided polygon.[23]

Our theory identifies specific factors that we expect to impact agency discretion. Of course, other theories might identify different subsets of variables acting through different political processes, which could also have significant impact on legislative and rule-making outcomes. Thus, the social science approach is to define a series of smaller, theory-driven empirical models rather than the more totalitarian kitchen sink models that typify much of big data analysis. This reduction in scope may indeed fail to incorporate certain variables that have surprising and significant impact on the phenomenon of interest. In return, however, the researcher is better able to infer important factors that drive the political process and hence evaluate alternative institutional structures.

NEW MACHINE LEARNING TECHNIQUES TO ANALYZE FINANCIAL REGULATION DATA

Our purpose is to apply computational data science methods, such as NLP and ML algorithms, to financial regulation in order to illustrate how these tools can be used to develop robust indicators of regulatory structure that previously have been limited by dependence on manual coding methods alone. Combining traditional methods with these new computational techniques offers a much richer process to both analyze and understand financial regulation.

Table 2 compares observational methods and data science techniques along four main criteria: coding legislation, structuring data sets, analysis, and internal validity. The table illustrates the limitations of manual rules–based coding methods and the ways in which these new techniques, when appropriately applied, can provide robustness checks on observational studies. Overall, computational analysis helps lessen error, reduce variance, find additional variables and patterns (data features), and add predictive power to models.[24]

Let us consider the example of the Dodd-Frank Act, which covers the activities that financial institutions can undertake, how these institutions will be regulated, and the regulatory architecture itself. The law contains 686 major provisions, of which 322 delegate authority to some 46 federal agencies. In addition, the act has a total of 341 constraints across 11 dif-

---

23. Delegation provisions can be even further disaggregated into delegation to the executive, the states, or the courts. For our study, which focuses on only a subset of these data, a neural net trained on first-order interactive effects would yield over 15 million predictive variables.

24. Lewis's (2014) study shows that manual coding using statistical quality control methods achieves higher levels of inter-annotator consistency, recall, and precision than it is commonly given credit for in the information retrieval literature. Nevertheless, he finds that text classification trained on fewer than 1,000 examples performs even better. When text classification is tuned to hit the same recall target as manual review, it allows fewer laws to be manually checked by lawyers, for a substantial cost reduction.

Table 2. Comparison of Observational Study and New Machine Learning Method

	Observational			Machine Learning	
	Process	Disadvantages		Process	Advantages
Coding congressional bills	Define coding rules	High labor and time costs		Use NLP to recode delegation and constrain provisions for each bill	Efficiency improved
	Assign multiple coders	Coder bias		Represent data in various feature representations as words, semantic units, relations, dependency structures, etc.	Consistency in coding improved
	Conduct multiple-round checks for coding consistency				Detect implicit/latent keywords Scalability
Structuring high-dimensional data set	Use factor analysis to construct discretion index	Limited in assigning meaningful and precise weights		Many ML algorithms can easily handle high-dimensional data	Feature selection algorithms allow us to reduce dimensions easily
	Use pivot table to structure raw data sets				

	Column 1	Column 2	Column 3
Analysis	Hypothesis testing, regression analysis, and finding correlations on dependent and independent variables (combine the panoply of independent variables in a single analysis)	Limitation in ability to test many hypotheses Meaningful manual analysis of correlations on thousands of variable is difficult Highly dependent on scaling and sensitive to outliers	Compare the accuracy with text features, with human coding rules features, with the combination of human coding rules and text features, and with the feature selection algorithms (Take account of the raw words of legal bills and explore word relations and other sets of features that otherwise would have been hard to encode manually)	Not limited by the data volume Go beyond coding rules to quantify each bill to build discretion model More precise feature selection We can optimize model complexity and predict capacity
Internal validity	Low	Miss the embedded structure of the data and important variables	High	No functional form imposed Low generalization error No overfit

Source: Authors' compilation.

ferent categories, and creates 22 new agencies. If we process the text of this law by the coding method detailed in the previous section, data annotators, trained in political economy theories, would read and code the provisions based on the rulebook provided. In effect, coders would have to read 30,000 words—the length of a short novel. Unlike a novel, however, legislation is written in complex legal language, which must be interpreted correctly and in painstaking detail. Consequently, there is the possibility that data annotators will introduce noise when coding laws.

Data Representation Using Natural Language Processing

Natural language processing is a subfield of computer science that deals with making machines process human (natural) language in the form of text and speech. The algorithms invented in NLP allow machines to better decipher the meaning of text (language understanding) and generate text that conforms with natural language grammar (language generation). For our purposes of processing legislation enacted by Congress, techniques of language understanding are relevant. One important topic in natural language understanding is data representation: how can we best and most appropriately represent text and speech data for machines to understand, and what information can we then extract from a given data structure?

The following text encoding and representation methods are used in NLP:

- *Bag of words:* A bag of words model represents text as a feature vector, where each feature is a word count or weighted word count.
- *Tag sequences:* Sentences or chunks of text are tagged with various information, such as parts of speech (POS) tags or named entities (NEs), which can be used to further process the text.
- *Graphs:* Laws or paragraphs of the laws can be represented in graphs where nodes can model sentences, entities, paragraphs, and connections that represent relations between them.
- *Logical forms:* This is a sequence of words mapped into an organized structure that encodes the semantics of the word sequence.

These methods can be applied to represent text, thereby allowing machines to extract additional information from the words (surface forms) of the documents. Depending on the problem being addressed, one or more of these tools may be useful. We next explain the representation form adopted for our computational analyses.

Computational Analyses: Data Science Methods

We have described the regression models and identified the key independent variables that correlate with the discretion index, defined as $D * (1 - C)$, where D is the delegation ratio and C is the constraint index. We should note that the process discussed earlier is a standard political economy approach to testing hypotheses. In this section, we explore data science methods and identify the techniques best suited to address the limitations of traditional observational methods. In particular, we seek not only to pinpoint important independent variables but also to determine the factors or "features" that predict agency discretion. Identifying the key features, words, or word patterns that predict the level of agency discretion in a given law helps refine and develop better proxies for institutional structure.[25]

We next describe the computational model for predicting the level of agency discretion using NLP and machine learning techniques. We gain significant leverage in building predictive models of agency discretion by employing ad-

---

25. Unlike our earlier regression analysis, our purpose here is to find characteristics of the law itself that predict agency discretion. The computational analysis approach lets the data identify those policy features or attributes that most accurately predict outcomes rather than be limited to testing hypotheses about the impact of theoretically motivated independent explanatory variables. We argue that the two approaches—computational analysis and hypothesis testing—are opposite sides of the same coin.

vanced computational data science methods, including the following:

- We are not limited by the amount of data we can process.
- We are not limited to a handful of coding rules to quantify each law for building the discretion model.
- We can take account of the raw text of the law to explore word combinations and syntactic and dependency relations and identify other sets of features that otherwise would be difficult to encode manually.
- We can optimize model complexity and predictive capacity to obtain the optimal model for predicting agency discretion.

Text Classification

We frame the challenge of predicting the level of agency discretion in a given law as a classification problem. We denote the discretion rank as Rn, where n ranges from 0 to N. N is the total number of ranks used to tag individual laws for the discretion rank.

The discretion rank R in a given law is a subjective measure of how much discretionary authority is granted to the agency in that law only. It is coded from 0 to 5, with 0 indicating that no discretionary authority is given to executive agencies to regulate financial markets and 5 meaning that the law delegates significant discretionary authority.[26]

Processing the Raw Text Data of Individual Laws

We need to represent each individual law in a form suitable for machine learning algorithm to take as inputs. We first convert the raw text of an individual law in feature representation format. For the current analysis, we convert the text of the financial regulation laws into word vectors using a vector space model. We take the following steps to convert text into feature vectors:

Step 1—Data cleaning: For each law, we first clean the text to remove any words that do not represent core content, including meta-information such as dates, public law (P.L.) number, and other meta-data that may have been added by *CQ*.

Step 2—Tokenization: After cleaning the data, we tokenize the text. Tokenization in NLP involves splitting a block of text into a set of tokens (words) by expanding abbreviations ("Mr." becomes "Mister"), expanding words ("I've" becomes "I have"), splitting punctuation from adjoining words ("He said," becomes "He said"), and splitting text using a delimiter such as a white space ("bill was submitted" becomes "(bill) (was) (submitted)"). Tokenization is language-dependent and more difficult in those languages in which word segmentation is not as straightforward as splitting the text at white spaces.

Step 3—Normalization: Once the text is tokenized, we must then normalize the data. The normalization of data requires having consistent tokenization across the same set of words. For example, if we have three different tokens to represent the World Health Organization— "WHO," "W.H.O.," and "World Health Organization"—normalization will map all three into one tokenized form such as "World Health Organization." The normalization step also converts currency, dates, and times into standard formats, such as converting "$24.4 million" into "24 million and 400,000 U.S. dollars." Different representations of dates may be converted into a single canonical form.

Step 4—Vocabulary: To represent text in the form of feature vectors, we need to find the to-

---

26. Note that the rank of discretion measure is distinct from the discretion index discussed earlier, which is constructed using detailed coding rules. The rank of discretion measure is determined to be significant when a law gives an agency or agencies authority in a sector or area of activity where none existed previously. Examples include the authority given to the Commodity Futures Trading Commission to regulate derivatives, or the creation of a single agency, such as the Consumer Financial Protection Bureau, to oversee consumer protection across the entire financial sector. The key criteria adopted in assigning a law to one of the five categories are: (1) the importance of the legislation, (2) the impact on the affected industry, and (3) the scope of applicable agency discretion. For example, the Bank Holding Company Act of 1956 gave the Federal Reserve authority to decide which companies could become a bank holding company. In this case, the act was assigned to category 3, as the agency's discretion applied only to a subset of firms.

tal vocabulary of the corpus appended with the additional vocabulary of the language. Any words not in the vocabulary will be considered out-of-vocabulary words, which tend to reduce the accuracy of the model. Hence, it is desirable to have the complete vocabulary of the domain for which we are building the model. We can excerpt vocabulary by extracting all unique tokens from the corpus of the text. If our corpus is small, we can also find pre-extracted vocabulary in a large set of English words, such as the Gigaword corpus.

Step 5—Vector representation: Once we have defined the vocabulary, we can treat each word as adding one dimension in the feature vector that represents a block of text. Thus, let Li be the vector representation for law i. $Li = w1, w2, \ldots, wn$, where wk represents the existence of word wk in the law Li. Let us take an example piece of text from the Dodd-Frank Act, contained in section 1506. $Li =$ *"the definition of core deposits for the purpose of calculating the insurance premiums of banks."* Let N be the total vocabulary size. The vector representation for this law Li will consist of a vector of length N where all values are set to zero except for the words that exist in law Li. The total vocabulary size N tends to be significantly bigger than the number of unique words that exist in a given law, so the vector tends to be very sparse. Hence, the vector Vi for law Li is stored in sparse form such that only non-zero dimensions of the vector are actually stored. The vector of Li will be

$$Vi = \{definition = 1.0, representation = 1.0, core = 1.0, purpose = 1.0, calculate = 1.0, insurance = 1.0, premium = 1.0, bank = 1.0\}. \quad (1)$$

This is a binary vector representation of the text Li. We can in fact keep track of the word count in the given law Li and store counts in the vector instead of storing the binary number representing whether the word is present in the law. Correspondingly, this generates a multinomial vector representation of the same text. If we take the entire Dodd-Frank Act as Lq, rather than sample text, and store counts for each word, we yield the vector representation of the act as:

$$Vq = \{sec = 517.0, financial = 304.0, securities = 106.0, requires = 160.0, federal = 154.0, requirements = 114.0, \ldots, inspection = 2.0\}. \quad (2)$$

*Step 6—TF * IDF transformation:* Once we represent the laws containing the law in raw word vector format, we can improve the vector representation format by weighting each dimension of the vector with a corresponding inverse document frequency (IDF) (Robertson and Jones 1976). An IDF transformation takes account of giving less weight to words that occur across all laws. For example, if the word "house" occurs frequently in all laws, then it has less distinguishing power for a given class than "SEC," which may occur less frequently but is strongly tied to a given rank of agency discretion level. We reweight all the dimensions of our vector Lq by multiplying them with the corresponding IDF score for the given word. We can obtain IDF scores for each word wi by creating an IDF vector that can be computed by equation 3.

$$IDF(w_i) = \log \frac{N}{count-of-Doc-with-w_i} \quad (3)$$

where N is the total number of laws in the corpus and $count-of-Doc-with-w_i$ is the total number of laws with the word wi. If the word wi occurs in all laws, then the IDF score is 0.

Naive Bayes Model

Many different machine learning algorithms are used in text classification problems. One of the most commonly applied algorithms is a naive Bayes method. We build a naive Bayes model for predicting discretion rank for each of the laws y. As noted earlier, the discretion rank that we are attempting to predict is based on subjectively labeled data for discretion. In contrast, the discretion index computed earlier is based on the delegation ratio and the constraint index. The discretion rank is a subjective ranking of laws (Ri), ranging from 0 to 5, where 0 represents no discretion and 5 represents the highest level of discretion. For ML models, subjective judgment is the gold standard that algorithms have to predict (a standard practice when ML models are built).

Thus, we construct computational models to predict the discretion rank (the "true" subjective rankings [Ri]) instead of the discretion index. With this in mind, let Ri be the discretion rank that we are trying to predict for a given law y.[27]

We need to compute $p(Ri|y)$ for each of the ranks (discretion ranks) and find the rank Ri; we begin by obtaining $p(Ri|y)$ from equation 4:

$$p(R_i|y) = \frac{p(R_i)p(y|R_i)}{p(y)} \quad (4)$$

To find the best rank Ri, we compute the argmax on the class variable:

$$i* = \max p(Ri/y). \quad (5)$$

To compute $p(Ri|y)$, we use Bayes's rule to obtain $p(Ri|y) = (p(y|R_i)*p(R_i))/p(y)$. Since our task is to find argmax on Ri, we simply need to locate Ri with the highest probability that can be ignored. Because the term $p(y)$ is constant across all different ranks of discretion, it is typically ignored.

Next, we describe how we can compute $p(y|Ri)$ and $p(Ri)$, which is the prior probability of class Ri. This term is computed on the training set by counting the number of occurrences of each discretion rank. In other words, if N is the total number of laws in training and Ni is the number of laws from a given discretion rank i, then $p(Ri) = Ni-Ni/N$.

To compute the probability $p(y|Ri)$, we assume that law y comprises the following words $y = \{w1, w2, \ldots, wn\}$, where n is the number of words in the law y. We make a conditional independence assumption that allows us to express $p(y|Ri) = p(w1, \ldots, wn|Ri)$ as

$$p(w_i, \ldots w_n|R_i = \Pi_{j=1}^{n} Pw_j|Ri) \quad (6)$$

We compute $P(w_j|R_i)$ by counting the number of times word w_j appears in all of the laws in the training corpus from rank R_i. Generally, add-one smoothing is used to address the words that never occur in the training document. Add-one smoothing is defined as follows: Let Nij be the number of times word wj is found in rank Ri and let $P(wj|Ri)$ be defined by equation 7, where V is the size of the vocabulary.

$$P(w_j|R_i) = \frac{N_{ij}+1}{\Sigma_i N_{ij}+v} \quad (7)$$

Given a test law y, for each word wj in y we look up the probability $P(wj|Ri)$ in the test laws and substitute it into equation 7 to compute the probability of y being predicted as Ri.

For the remainder of this section, we describe the naive Bayes model we built from different sets of features so as to be able to compare the performance of our model in various settings.

Naive Bayes model 1: The first naive Bayes model is based on the law vectors in which the data are all the text found in the financial regulatory laws, which includes more than 12,000 distinct words. Each word is a parameter that must be estimated across each of the six discretion ranks. We took the raw text of the laws and converted it into vectors, as described in the previous section, and estimated the parameters of the naive Bayes model. This model produced an accuracy of 37 percent with an F-measure of 0.38.

Our baseline system is a model that predicts rank 0 for all laws. Absent any other information, the best prediction for a law is a rank that has the highest prior probability, which is 0.26 for rank 0. We should note that naive Bayes model 1 based solely on text features did better

---

27. The goal of the ML model is to learn patterns that generalize well for unseen data. To do this, we use the model to predict the answer on the evaluation data set and then compare the predicted target to the actual answer. To evaluate the performance of a given ML model in predicting agency discretion, for example, we first assign each law a label or rank Ri, ranging from 0 to 6 (ground truth). The value for the discretion rank is assigned by expert evaluators and is deemed the target answer. It is important to note that each law is assigned a category or rank level of discretion independent of the discretion index calculated earlier. Second, we compare the predictions yielded by the ML models against the baseline or target value. Finally, we compute a summary metric; here we use the F-statistic, which indicates the accuracy of alternative models in correctly classifying each law relative to the baseline. See Amazon Web Services, *Amazon Machine Learning Developer Guide*, http://docs.aws.amazon.com/machine-learning/latest/dg/what-is-amazon-machine-learning.html (accessed August 9, 2016).

Table 3. Class and Prior Probability for the Six Ranks of the Discretion Index

Class	Prior Probability
0	0.26
1	0.14
2	0.25
3	0.24
4	0.08
5	0.07

Source: Authors' compilation.

than the baseline model by 11 percent. Table 3 shows the prior probabilities for the six ranks of the discretion rank.

Naive Bayes model 2: We first compared the model with features extracted from the raw text derived from the coding rules outlined earlier. We took the same set of laws and their corresponding coding rules as features. We identified more than forty features from the coding rules, including the number of provisions dealing with delegation; constraints such as reporting requirements, exemptions, and appointment power limits; the number of major provisions, the total number of constraint types, and so on. These coding rules are detailed in the guidebook found in the data appendix.

We next created a naive Bayes model using these hand-labeled coding rules as features. Naive Bayes is a general classification algorithm that can take any type of feature vectors as inputs. For model 2, we again estimated the parameters employing the same set of laws that we used to estimate the parameters for building model 1 and produced an accuracy of 30 percent and *F*-measure of 0.40. Interestingly, the raw text model produced a higher level of accuracy than the model built solely from the coding rules.[28]

Naive Bayes model 3: The third model combines the purely raw text approach of examining all of the laws and the manual approach of examining all the laws from the coding rules. We again estimated the parameters described earlier. This model produced an accuracy of 41 percent and an *F*-measure of 0.42. These results indicate that a combination of raw text and manual approaches performs better than either individual approach.

Naive Bayes model 4: The number of parameters for model 1 is almost the same size as the vocabulary of the corpus, while the total number of parameters for model 2 equals the number of manually labeled coding rules. It is likely that the raw text-based features can be overwhelming for a small number of manually labeled features. Therefore, we built a fourth naive Bayes model where we ran a feature selection algorithm on the combined set of features.

Feature selection algorithms select a subset of features based either on different constraints or on the maximization of a given function. We used a correlation-based feature selection algorithm that selects features that are highly correlated with the given class but have low correlation among themselves, as described in Hall (1998). The feature selection algorithm picked up a feature set containing forty-seven features, including a few features from the manually produced coding rules and a few word-based features. Some of the words selected by the feature selection algorithm for discretion rank include: "auditor," "deficit," "depository," "executives," "federal," "prohibited," "provisions," "regulatory," and "restrict."

Model 4 produced the highest level of accuracy at 67 percent with an *F*-measure of 0.68. If the model had no predictive power, then the random assignment of each law to a given rank would be approximately 16 percent. The feature selection improved the accuracy of classifying each law into the correct rank by fourfold. A key reason for such an increase in accuracy was that after discarding a number of word-based features, the smaller feature selection set that remained allowed us to better estimate the parameters with our data set. The best model produced a high degree of accuracy

---

28. However, when the data are as highly skewed as they are here, *F*-measure may be more appropriate, since it takes into account both precision and the recall or sensitivity of the analysis. In this case, the *F*-statistics for the rules-based manual coding method performed better than the unstructured computer-generated features.

Table 4. Naive Bayes Models

Feature Type	Accuracy (%)	F-Measure
Model 1: computer-generated text features (C)	36.66	0.38
Model 2: manually coded variables/features (M)	30.00	0.40
Model 3: C + M	40.83	0.42
Model 4: feature selection (C + M)	66.66	0.68

Source: Authors' compilation.

only after careful feature selection and careful model design.

Table 4 summarizes the results of the four models.

CONCLUSION

In this chapter, we have combined observational methods with new computational data science techniques to understand a fundamental problem in political economy—the institutional structure of financial sector regulation. The centerpiece of the study is a database of all financial regulation laws enacted since 1950. The analysis has focused on the delegation of discretionary authority to regulatory agencies with respect to financial sector laws. To improve our estimate of agency discretion and facilitate hypothesis testing, we employ both the observational method and data sciences techniques.

Computational data science captures complex patterns and interactions that are not easily recognized by coding rules. In particular, we apply new NLP and ML techniques to analyze text-based data on congressional legislation to test theories of regulatory design. For instance, these computational methods allow us to represent all the text in a given law as a feature vector where each feature represents a word or weighted terms for words, thereby collaring the relevant terms for different discretion ranks. Furthermore, we can use parsers to find syntactic and dependency parses of sentences that can help quantify intricate connections between the phrases of a sentence with respect to a given implied meaning of a provision. Each of these techniques provides potential improvements over manual coding from a set of defined rules. Yet these computational models rely on the critical data initially produced by subject matter experts to inform or "seed" the model and train complex algorithms. Therefore, big data techniques are not a replacement for observational studies; rather, they should be seen as complements.

Combining both the observational studies and the new machine learning approaches enables us to go beyond the limitations of both methods and offer a more precise interpretation of the determinants of financial regulatory structure. A research strategy that uses more than one technique of data collection can improve the validity of analyzing the high-dimensional data sets commonly found in political economy studies. By illustrating how triangulating different methods can enhance our understanding of important substantive public policy concerns, this paper offers a new path.

REFERENCES

Alesina, Alberto, and Guido Tabellini. 2007. "Bureaucrats or Politicians? Part I: A Single Policy Task." *American Economic Review* 97(1): 169–79.

Alonso, Ricardo, and Niko Matouschek. 2008. "Optimal Delegation." *Review of Economic Studies* 75(1): 259–93.

Barth, James R., Gerard Caprio Jr., and Ross Levine. 2006. *Rethinking Banking Regulation: Till Angels Govern*. New York: Cambridge University Press.

Bendor, Jonathan, and Adam Meirowitz. 2004. "Spatial Models of Delegation." *American Political Science Review* 98(2): 293–310.

Carlson, Melissa D. A., and R. Sean Morrison. 1999."Study Design, Precision, and Validity in Observational Studies." *Journal of Palliative Medicine* 12(1): 77–82.

Clark, William Roberts, and Matt Golder. 1995. "Big Data, Casual Inference, and Formal Theory: Contradictory Trends in Political Science?" *PS: Political Science & Politics APSC* 48(1): 65-70.

Epstein, David and Sharyn O'Halloran. 1999. *Delegating Powers*. New York: Cambridge University Press.

Fiorina, Morris P. 1977. "An Outline for a Model of Party Choice." *American Journal of Political Science* 21(3): 601-25.

———. 1982. "Legislative Choice of Regulatory Forms: Legal Process or Administrative Process?" *Public Choice* 39(1): 33-66.

Gailmard, Sean. 2009. "Discretion Rather than Rules: Choice of Instruments to Control Bureaucratic Policy making." *Political Analysis* 17(1): 25-44.

Gailmard, Sean, and John W. Patty. 2007. "Slackers and Zealots: Civil Service, Policy Discretion, and Bureaucratic Expertise." *American Journal of Political Science* 51(4): 873-89.

———. 2012. "Formal Models of Bureaucracy." *Annual Review of Political Science* 15(1): 353-77.

Groll, Thomas, Sharyn O'Halloran, and Geraldine McAllister. 2014. "Delegation and the Regulation of Finance in the United States Since 1950." Working paper. New York: Columbia University.

Hall, M. A. 1998. "Correlation-Based Feature Subset Selection for Machine Learning." PhD thesis. University of Waikato.

Hiriart, Yolande, and David Martimort. 2012. "How Much Discretion for Risk Regulators?" *The RAND Journal of Economics* 43(2): 283-314. doi: 10.1111/j.1756-2171.2012.001666.x.

Kroszner, Randall S., and Philip E. Strahan. 1999. "What Drives Deregulation? Economics and Politics of the Relaxation of Bank Branching Restrictions." *Quarterly Journal of Economics* 114(4): 1437-67.

Lapinski, John S. 2008. "Policy Substance and Performance in American Lawmaking, 1877-1994." *American Journal of Political Science* 52(2): 235-51.

Lewis, David. 2014. "Supervised Learning in Civil Litigation: A Case Study." Working paper. Washington, D.C.: American Association for the Advancement of Science.

Lowi, Theodore. 1979. *The End of Liberalism: The Second Republic of the United States*. 2nd ed. New York: W. W. Norton.

Macey, Jonathan R., Geoffrey P. Miller, and Richard Scott Carnell. 2001. *Banking Law and Regulation*. New York: Aspen Publishers.

Maskin, Eric, and Jean Tirole. 2004. "The Politician and the Judge: Accountability in Government." *American Economic Review* 94(4): 1034-54.

Mayhew, David R. 2005. *Divided We Govern: Party Control, Lawmaking, and Investigations, 1946-2002*. New Haven, Conn.: Yale University Press.

McCubbins, Mathew D. 1985. "The Legislative Design of Regulatory Structure." *American Journal of Political Science* 29(4): 721.

McCubbins, Matthew D., Roger Noll, and Barry Weingast. 1987. "Administrative Procedures as Instruments of Political Control." *Journal of Law, Economics, and Organization* 3(2): 243-77.

———. 1989. "Structure and Process, Politics and Policy: Administrative Arrangements and the Political Control of Agencies." *Virginia Law Review* 75(2): 431.

McCubbins, Matthew D., and Thomas Schwartz. 1984. "Congressional Oversight Overlooked: Police Patrols Versus Fire Alarms." *American Journal of Science* 28(1): 165.

Melumad, Nahum D., and Toshiyuki Shibano. 1991. "Communication in Settings with No Transfers." *Economics* 22(2): 173.

Moe, Terry M. 1984. "The New Economics of Organization." *American Journal of Political Science* 28(4): 739.

Morgan, Donald. 2002. "Rating Banks: Risk and Uncertainty in an Opaque Industry." *American Economic Review* 92(4): 874-88.

Philippon, Thomas, and Ariell Reshef. 2009. "Wages and Human Capital in the U.S. Financial Industry: 1909-2006." Working Paper 14644. Cambridge, Mass.: National Bureau of Economic Research.

Robertson, S. E., and K. Sparck Jones. 1976. "Relevance Weighting of Search Terms." *Journal of the American Society for Information Science* 27(3): 129-46.

Stigler, George J. 1971. "The Theory of Economic Regulation." *Bell Journal of Economics* 2(1): 3-21.

Sundquist, James L. 1981. *The Decline and Resurgence of Congress*. Washington, D.C.: Brookings Institution.

Tirole, Jean. 2006. *The Theory of Corporate Finance*. Princeton, N.J.: Princeton University Press.

Titiunik, Rocío. 2015. "Can Big Data Solve the Fundamental Problem of Causal Inference?" *PS: Political Science & Politics* 48(1): 75-79.

Volden, Craig. 2002. "A Formal Model of the Politics of Delegation in a Separation of Powers System."

American Journal of Political Science 46(1): 111–33.

Volden, Craig, and Alan Wiseman. 2011. "Formal Approaches to the Study of Congress." In *The Oxford Handbook of the American Congress*, edited by Eric Schickler and Frances E. Lee. Oxford: Oxford University Press.

Wiseman, Alan E. 2009. "Delegation and Positive-Sum Bureaucracies." *Journal of Politics* 71(3): 998–1014.